Setting Healthy Boundaries

A Guide to Improving Your Self-Esteem, Building Self-Confidence, and Setting Yourself Free

Mary Ann Hill

ISBN 978-87-974306-0-6

Table of Contents

Introduction

Are your relationships healthy? Do you feel in control of your life? Or do you have a hard time saying no? Perhaps you get angry often? If any of these resonate with you, maybe you need to set some boundaries.

Boundaries are essential to our well-being. They protect us from being used, manipulated, or taken advantage of. They also help us take care of ourselves emotionally and physically. When we establish and maintain healthy boundaries, we gain a sense of control in our lives and help to create healthy relationships.

Boundaries were something I struggled with my whole life. I was always a people pleaser and had a hard time saying no. As a result, I often found myself in unhealthy situations or relationships throughout my life.

As a child, it started with my parents—as I'm sure it starts for most of us. I was afraid to disappoint them. So, I would go along with my parents and do whatever they wanted, even if it wasn't in my best interest. This led to me being taken advantage of and not understanding how to take care of myself.

In my teenage years, this pattern grew out of control. I worked hard for good grades, kept the house clean, and even helped pay the bills at a young age to "impress" them. This pattern continued with my friends. I joined activities I didn't want to do, went to parties that made me uncomfortable, and watched boring movies just to fit in. This led to me getting into some unhealthy and even dangerous situations.

During my teen years, I felt a lot of anger. I held resentment towards my friends and family—how come I always came last? My adult years followed the same pattern—pleasing partners or employers, even at my own expense. It wasn't until I sat down with a friend, broken and in tears, that I made a connection. My friend told me something that I wasn't able to shake loose. She told me that people put me last because I put myself last. I show everyone else that they're more important—that my boundaries don't matter because I willingly bend to their rules.

After that day, I took a step back from my relationships and started re-evaluating my wants and needs. Happiness and peace were unfamiliar states to me, but I longed for them, and I was willing to do anything to achieve them. Over the course of a few months, I became more in tune with myself. I tapped into my inner child and worked on healing my wounds.

As I understood myself better, I realized the true impact of not having boundaries. I saw how my lack of boundaries had led to me being taken advantage of, manipulated, and controlled. I also realized that it was preventing me from having healthy and fulfilling relationships. Instead, I ended up in relationships that were based on power struggles and manipulation.

However, as I started implementing boundaries, I noticed a drastic change. My social circle changed, but so did my confidence. When you surround yourself with the right people, your aura changes with them. Your experiences change, and you feel more at peace with those who support your growth. I experienced some backlash and even struggled as I searched for my independence, but I would never be the person sharing my story with you today if I hadn't.

So if you're struggling with boundary issues, know that you're not alone. And it's never too late to learn how to set boundaries. In this book, we'll explore what boundaries are, why they're important, and how to start setting them in your own life.

If you're unfamiliar with setting boundaries or lack the self-confidence to do so, this book is for you.

We'll explore:

- What boundaries are, and why they're important.

- How to set boundaries with yourself and others.

- How to identify and overcome your triggers.
- How to build self-esteem and self-confidence.
- How to communicate your boundaries to others.
- And much more!

By the end of this book, you will have a better understanding of what healthy boundaries look like and how to start setting them in your life. So let's get started!

Chapter 1:

Working With Yourself—the First Steps

Setting boundaries is crucial for yourself and your relationships. Having boundaries in place will help you identify when and where to say yes or no. You use these restrictions to help you establish the limits of your responsibilities and your tolerance for others' behavior.

However, when setting boundaries, understanding who you are and what makes you tick is crucial. If you don't understand how you work or how to work within your limitations, then you might set the wrong boundaries. Or you might fail to enforce the right ones, causing you to feel more anguish. By considering all areas of your life, including career, family, health, relationships, and finances, you can determine your values. Then develop a set of boundaries that's right for you.

At the heart of setting these boundaries is being able to say "no." This can be a tough but necessary skill to learn to have healthy relationships and protect your well-being. To say "no," though, you have to know what to say "no" to and how to say "no" when faced with a challenge.

The True Importance of Developing Yourself

Everyone has different boundaries. Some people may be more comfortable with certain interactions, like a greeting hug or dark joke. Others may not be. You are free to be who you want—there's no right or wrong way to be. However, it's important to consider your values and what you're comfortable with when setting boundaries. Not to mention, a huge part of setting boundaries is your self-esteem and confidence.

When you have confidence, you'll find it easier to deal with situations or interactions that may be difficult. You'll also feel more comfortable setting boundaries. You know you can voice your needs and wants without fear of judgment or repercussions. As you continue to develop yourself, it's important to continue evolving. This can mean adjusting your boundaries as needed as you grow and change as a person.

In the end, though, the first step to setting any boundary is always the same: Knowing yourself. This leads to confidence and self-esteem, which help you form the boundaries that are right for you.

How You Are Right Now

When you're ready to set boundaries, first determine where you are as a person. What qualities do you have, and where do you struggle? Are you confident in your abilities and clear on what you want out of life? Or do you worry others will judge or disappoint you? Are you struggling because you have trouble communicating your needs and desires effectively? Or is it that you feel like others are taking advantage of you or manipulating your boundaries due to low self-esteem or a lack of confidence?

Once you have a better understanding of the underlying causes of our problem, you can begin to work on developing effective strategies for change. For instance, if a lack of self-esteem is your concern, you might work on developing more positive affirmations, setting better boundaries with yourself, and practicing effective communication skills.

Or if it's a lack of confidence that's holding you back, you might try pursuing activities or hobbies that help boost your sense of self-worth and self-esteem. If you struggle to know what and where your boundaries are, you might seek the help of a therapist or coach, who can work with you to identify your needs and goals.

As you evaluate yourself, think about the different areas of your life. These can include work, relationships, health, finances, and more. What is most important to you within each area? What areas need more work? For example, if you value your health, what boundaries do you need to set to make sure that it continues to be a priority?

Or if you have boundaries in place already, like setting limits on the time you spend with a negative friend, think about where they could be improved. Maybe you can stop contact with the person completely? When you've taken an internal inventory of your positive and negative qualities, you can work on improving them to enhance your self-esteem.

Here are some common qualities people may lack that can affect their self-esteem and confidence:

- **Not feeling good enough**: Many people struggle with feelings of insecurity or a lack of confidence, especially in their relationships. They may feel as though they're not a good enough partner or that they're lacking as an employee. They may see themselves as "failures" and believe they cannot live up to the expectations of others. However, building up this self-confidence is key to being able to set boundaries in your life. One strategy that can help is positive affirmations, where you say positive things to yourself on a regular basis.

- **Not knowing what they want**: If you don't know what your values or triggers are, then it's tough to set and maintain boundaries. Gaining clarity and positive introspection is crucial to being successful with your boundary building. One way to get clarity is through journaling or meditation, where you reflect on your values and goals and then write or think about what you need to do to achieve them.

- **Fear of disappointing others**: If you lacked boundaries, you were likely a people pleaser. You want others to be happy, as long as they don't have too much of your experience. As a result, being fearful of upsetting someone else or of being judged for your choices can make saying no when needed a challenging task. Remember that you are not obligated to fulfill someone else's needs if they do not align with your own.

- **Not knowing how to say "no"**: As I mentioned at the beginning of the chapter, saying "no" is crucial to setting boundaries. People will try to cross your boundaries. In fact, they probably already are, but you haven't figured out where or how to say "no." However, by practicing effective communication skills and learning to be assertive, you can develop the strength to say "no." This can include reframing your self-talk, practicing visualization, or even role-playing.

Other common traits of low self-esteem are tendencies toward perfectionism, staying in isolation, and overworking. Regardless of how you feel in terms of confidence and self-esteem, remember that these are all qualities that can be improved with practice and time. When you start to set boundaries for yourself, you'll find it easier to maintain your well-being, both personally and professionally. Ultimately, the key is to stay committed to your boundaries and take action in ways that feel right for you.

The Way That You Need to Be

Once you've evaluated yourself and identified areas that need work, it's time to consider the way you want or need to be. For instance, if you lack boundaries with your friends or family, get over-involved, or feel taken advantage of, think about the changes you need to make to set boundaries.

This may include limiting your time with certain people and being more assertive about your needs and wants. You may find it helpful to practice self-care as you set these boundaries. Focusing on activities can help you feel happy and fulfilled while taking care of yourself. This can involve working on your self-talk and understanding what your triggers are.

Some common positive traits of high self-esteem and confidence are being honest with yourself, knowing your values and goals, and feeling secure in your decisions. With these qualities under your belt, you'll be able to begin setting healthy boundaries that help maintain your well-being and happiness for years to come.

Practice Acceptance: What We Want Might Not Always Be the Best Thing for Us

Our brains are brilliant tools that can help us navigate life and make choices. However, sometimes our brains can trick us into making critical decisions or believing in thoughts that aren't true. This can occur when setting boundaries because we might be tempted to engage even if we know that it's not in our best interests. For example, we may want to spend time with a friend even if we're feeling burned out and need some alone time. Or we may want to say "yes" to that last-minute work meeting even if we're already overcommitted.

The key to setting boundaries is knowing yourself well enough to recognize when you might make a choice that's not in your best interests. This means being honest with yourself about what you want and need. Trust that your feelings matter as much as anyone else's. When you accept that wanting something doesn't equate to it being good for you, you'll be able to set boundaries like a pro.

Understanding the Importance of Positive Self Changes

While it's tough to change the way you think about yourself, there are many benefits to doing so. For example, changing your self-talk can help improve your confidence levels. This will prompt you to feel more fulfilled and satisfied with your life. Additionally, making time for activities like yoga or meditation may help you find balance in your personal and professional lives, which can also help you set better boundaries.

Overall, as humans, no one is perfect, but there are specific ways we can handle challenges, communicate effectively, and be mindful of our actions. By making positive changes from within, you'll be able to shift your mindset and establish healthy boundaries that help you navigate life with greater confidence and self-esteem.

How Positive Self-Changes Help Us in the Life

Positive self-changes can help us in many ways in our lives. For example, by learning how to be more assertive and set healthy boundaries with others, we are better able to communicate our needs. Then we can protect ourselves from situations or people that may harm us, such as emotional or verbal abuse.

This can also lead to more positive relationships with others, as we can establish clear expectations for how we want to be treated. Additionally, by working on self-care activities like exercise or meditation, we can improve our overall well-being. Overall, the goal is to adapt or enhance our qualities in a way that will promote stronger boundaries and higher self-esteem, which, in turn, will help us live our best lives.

What Types of Positive Changes Do We Need in Our Lives?

Some people might benefit from learning how to better manage their stress and anxiety. Others may want to focus on improving their social or communication skills. Additionally, taking time for activities like self-reflection and mindfulness can also be helpful in helping us identify areas in our lives where we may struggle and develop strategies for making positive changes.

Ultimately, the key to success in bringing positive change into your life is to focus on what works best for you personally. Whether this means working with a therapist or coach, participating in group support programs, or simply making minor changes in your daily routine, the important thing is that you are committed to your growth and well-being.

The Importance of Building up Self-Esteem, Confidence, and Positive Energy

As I mentioned above, self-esteem, confidence, and positive energy are all crucial components of having good boundaries. Without these things, it's difficult to assert yourself healthily and set healthy limits with others.

A lack of self-esteem and confidence can lead to feelings of isolation and loneliness. This may make it harder for us to cope with the challenges and demands of our daily lives. Additionally, it can make it difficult for us to set and maintain boundaries. Without self-esteem or confidence, it's easier for us to allow others to cross or manipulate our boundaries. This can come from the fear of being judged or rejected, or simply because we aren't sure what our needs are.

However, by building up our self-esteem and confidence through practices like positive affirmations, self-care activities, and regular reflection, we can better protect ourselves from unhealthy behaviors and relationships. This in turn helps us establish and maintain strong, healthy boundaries.

By cultivating positive energy within ourselves, we can feel more hopeful and optimistic about the future, which can give us the strength we need to set better boundaries and forge healthier relationships with others. Ultimately, whether you are working on building your self-esteem or increasing your level of positive energy, the key is to be kind and compassionate towards yourself and to stay committed to making these positive changes a part of your daily life.

Taking the Action

Once you complete an in-depth evaluation of your life and identify areas where you need to work on building stronger boundaries, the next step is to take action. "Taking action" could mean distinct steps for different people and could include situations like working with a therapist or coach to develop better coping skills and communication strategies or engaging in regular self-care activities like yoga or meditation.

Regardless of what approach you take, the key is to remain committed to your growth and be compassionate as you work towards building stronger and healthier boundaries in your life. With time and practice, you will see the positive changes that you desire, both in yourself and in your relationships with others.

Avoid Wasting Time and Start Making the Change Right Away

In other cases, we know what our boundaries are—whether from years of trial and error or from assessing our values and needs—but we struggle to actually set them in practice and maintain them.

If this is your situation, don't waste time. Implement the change right away. The longer you wait to implement your boundaries, the harder it can be to actually change your or someone else's behavior. If you wait too long to implement your limits, then others might think you're making random demands or being mean and unkind.

Second, if you procrastinate or continually put off these changes, then you could end up feeling even more frustrated or unhappy with yourself. By starting now and taking action every day towards building better boundaries in your life, you will reap the immediate benefits. Some basic action steps are:

- Engaging in regular self-care activities.
- Talking to a therapist or coach about ways to build up your self-esteem and confidence.
- Setting boundaries with friends, family, coworkers, or partners by communicating your needs clearly and respectfully

- Seeking out new hobbies or activities that bring you joy and help to strengthen your sense of self-worth.

Ultimately, the key is to start taking action today, no matter how small. By doing so and being persistent in your efforts over time, you will build healthy boundaries in all areas of your life.

How to Use This Book

For each chapter, we'll review the importance of boundaries throughout our lives (such as at home, work, school, etc.) and identify some common challenges that many of us face. We'll also offer practical strategies to help better manage your boundaries, including:

- Setting clear and specific limits with yourself and others.

- Focusing on your needs and wants, rather than what others expect of you.

- Identifying areas where your boundaries are being violated or threatened.

- Developing self-compassion and forgiveness to avoid getting caught up in blame or negative self-talk.

Additionally, we'll offer tips for maintaining your boundaries over time and overcoming obstacles that may arise. Whether you're facing challenges with relationships, conflict at work, or even managing difficult emotions like guilt or anger, this book will give you the tools, strategies, and guidance you need to build healthier boundaries and live a happier, more fulfilling life.

Following the Instructions

As you read through the chapters, take time to reflect on how you can implement the guidance and tips into your life. Pay particular attention to areas where you may struggle to set and maintain healthy boundaries. For instance, in which area do you struggle most: Friends or family, at work or school, or in other important relationships?

Take small steps each day towards building better boundaries. For example, start by simply paying attention to how you're feeling and what your needs are, without judging yourself or others. You might also want to set aside some time each week for self-care activities like journaling, exercise, or meditation.

Getting Ahead of the Common Pitfalls

This journey may not be an easy one. Especially if you're not accustomed to setting boundaries or speaking up for yourself. You may encounter some challenges along the way.

However, by being mindful and aware of how you're feeling and practicing patience and self-compassion, you can learn to overcome these obstacles and move forward with confidence. If you're aware of the common pitfalls, your triggers, and how they might manifest within you, you can better understand what you need to do in order to keep your boundaries strong and healthy.

Above all else, remember that the journey towards healthier boundaries is lifelong. It's not about perfection but rather about gradually building up your skills, confidence, and self-awareness over time.

What Are Common Hardships You Might Face During Your Journey Towards Healthier Boundaries?

As I mentioned, this might be an arduous process. It doesn't matter how old you are, how many years you've interacted with others, or what your background is—we all face challenges in setting and maintaining healthy boundaries.

Some of the common hardships that you might encounter include dealing with pushback or resistance from others when you alert them of your boundaries. You might experience guilt or shame after asserting yourself, especially if others speak out. Or you might struggle with your independence, and can't find time for self-care and maintenance.

Additionally, many people struggle with maintaining their boundaries over time, as well as managing negative emotions such as anger or frustration. To overcome these hurdles, it's important to practice self-compassion, remain patient with yourself and your progress, and take baby steps to accomplish your goals. In short, the journey towards healthier boundaries is a long and challenging one, but it's also a deeply rewarding one.

Overall, setting and maintaining healthy boundaries is a challenging but rewarding process that takes time and persistence. Whether you're struggling with relationships at work or school, navigating difficult emotions like guilt or shame, or simply trying to find time for self-care, remember that every step you take is an important one. With patience and compassion for yourself, you can learn to set healthy boundaries and create a more fulfilling life for yourself.

Chapter 2:

About Setting Boundaries

There's no denying that setting boundaries can be one of the most challenging aspects of any personal development journey. Whether it's saying "no" to something you don't want or having the confidence to stand up for yourself when someone is trying to walk all over you, setting boundaries can be terrifying but necessary if you want to live a balanced, healthy life.

While it's tough to master, setting boundaries doesn't have to be an impossible task. In fact, you can take several steps right now to help you get started and begin mastering the art of setting healthy boundaries for yourself. First, though, before we implement boundaries, let's review what boundaries are and their common misconceptions.

What Are Boundaries?

Simply put, "boundaries" are limits you set for yourself and others, both during the workday and in your personal life. They are defined by what you do or don't do on a daily basis. Setting boundaries can help you achieve greater control over your thoughts, actions, and emotions.

At their core, boundaries help establish a sense of safety and security in your relationships. They provide you with guidelines for how you want to be treated, both by yourself and others. While setting these limits may at first seem difficult or uncomfortable, having clear boundaries actually allows you to feel more confident and in control of your life and choices.

There are many common misconceptions about boundaries, such as the belief that they are controlling or rigid. You might be viewed as a "tight-ass" or strict. In reality, establishing healthy boundaries is all about expressing your values and needs in a way that works for you. It's not about trying to control other people or force them to act your way. Instead, it's about determining how you want to be treated and then communicating that clearly with others. How they choose to act is up to them, but what you will tolerate is not.

Examples of Implementing Boundaries

Boundaries and limits come wide and many. Here are just a few examples of how you might implement boundaries in your day-to-day life:

- Saying "no" to co-workers who ask you to take on additional responsibilities or tasks that you don't have the time and mental capacity for.

- Setting limits on the time you spend with friends and family who drain your energy or make you feel poorly about yourself.

- Establishing time limits on work-related tasks during off-hours, such as responding to emails or taking work calls after dinner.

- Saying "no" to your partner or spouse when they ask you to do something that makes you uncomfortable, rather than trying to avoid the conflict by agreeing.

- Determining who you're willing to interact with and what types of interactions you're willing to engage in on a daily basis.

While setting boundaries can be challenging at first, many tools and strategies can make the process easier and more effective. Some key steps include identifying your core values and defining what's important to you, communicating your needs clearly with others, and practicing self-care to maintain your mental and physical health. With the right approach, you can set boundaries that work for you and help you live a happier, more balanced life.

Why Do We Need Boundaries?

At its core, setting boundaries is about having healthy relationships. When you don't have strong boundaries in place, you may find that your relationships suffer. If you feel poorly about a relationship, then it's likely one-sided somehow. Boundaries can help make the relationship feel more balanced. If a person cannot respect your boundaries, then simply put, that's not someone you want or should have in your life. If they are unwilling to change, you will probably continue to feel bad about yourself or the relationship. You might also experience feelings of anger or resentment toward the other person, which can cause strain in your relationship. Boundaries are a matter of maintaining respect and trust between you and the person you're trying to set them with. It helps avoid the turmoil that can arise.

The Impact of Boundaries

Setting boundaries can be especially important for those who have experienced trauma or abuse, as it can help you reclaim your power and begin healing. For many people, setting boundaries can be a life-changing experience that allows them to feel more in control of their lives and better able to express themselves. Setting boundaries can help you become more resilient and able to handle stress, difficult emotions, and other challenges that come your way.

What Happens if You Lack Boundaries?

If you do not set boundaries for yourself, you may find that others take advantage of you and your time. You may feel exhausted and overwhelmed. For instance, if you do not set boundaries at work, you may overextend yourself and work long hours with little to no breaks. Or if you don't set clear boundaries in your relationships, your friends or romantic partners might constantly impose on your time and energy. You may also struggle to prioritize your own needs and desires, which can lead to feelings of guilt or shame. You may even experience burnout, depression, or other mental health issues because you neglected your own needs and goals.

The bottom line is that if you want to lead a happier, more fulfilling life and achieve your goals, it's crucial to set clear boundaries in all areas of your life. These boundaries allow you to determine the space you're comfortable working or interacting in. Then you can establish healthy limits that respect not only your own needs but those of others as well. So don't be afraid to set some boundaries and take charge of your personal development—the benefits are well worth it!

Importance of Boundaries in Personal and Professional Life

Setting boundaries is important both in our personal lives and in our professional careers. Many of us spend a lot of time at work, and it's important to have boundaries in place there too. Otherwise, you might allow your boss to take advantage of you or your co-workers to exert undue pressure on you to meet unrealistic deadlines.

For instance, setting boundaries can help you avoid feeling pressured to work long hours or giving in when your boss asks you to take on another last-minute project. In your personal life, setting boundaries can help you avoid getting pulled too much in one direction by your family members or feeling overwhelmed by the demands of others.

How Boundaries Might Change How We Exist in Our Society

The importance of setting boundaries can't be understated. When we have strong boundaries in place, it's easier to maintain healthy relationships. We can also avoid situations that might cause us stress or undue pressure. This allows us to live our lives in a way that feels more balanced and fulfilling, both at work and at home.

At the same time, boundaries aren't static. They may need to be adjusted over time as our lives and relationships change or in response to situations we encounter. However, healthy boundaries can change the way we interact and exist within our society positively. For example, having healthy boundaries can help us stand up for our own needs and beliefs, even in the face of social pressures or expectations from others. This can help us feel more confident and empowered, both professionally and personally.

How "What Society Might Think" Might Get Even More Important Than You Would Have Ever Thought

Society loves to stigmatize atypical behaviors and beliefs, so be aware of these potential judgments when setting boundaries. For instance, if you have strong political or moral convictions that you feel strongly about, these might not always be shared by others in your social circle. This could make it difficult to set boundaries around these issues without facing judgment or criticism from others.

At the same time, don't allow what others might think to be a determining factor in how we set our own boundaries. This means that even if there are negative judgments or perceptions about your behavior or beliefs, you should still stand up for yourself and speak out on those issues. It doesn't matter if an issue or concern doesn't resonate with your friends and family, nor does it matter if they don't approve of your choices.

Ultimately, setting boundaries can be a challenging process—but it's a process solely meant for you. By staying true to your values and needs, you can help maintain healthy relationships and avoid the negative judgment of others. And that is something that should be valued above all else in our society.

Aspects of Life That Are Mostly Up to You

Most people can control certain aspects of their lives, including what they do each day, who they interact with, and how they set and manage their boundaries. By exercising your agency in these areas, you can take back some of the power that has been taken from you by others. Below are the few areas of life that are in your control.

Behaviors

The way you behave is completely up to you. Sure, at times we may feel compelled to react in certain ways due to our circumstances or the actions of others, but at the end of the day, we always have a choice about how we behave. Whether it's taking a step back and responding rationally when you feel overwhelmed or angry, setting clear boundaries with co-workers who take advantage of your time or energy, or simply speaking up for yourself when others try to take advantage of you, your actions and behaviors are always within your control.

Some behaviors you can control are the following:

- Saying "no" when you need to, and setting limits on the time or energy you will devote to certain activities.
- Taking care of yourself physically and mentally by getting enough rest, eating a healthy diet, and taking time for self-care activities like meditation or exercise.
- Choosing how you spend your time and energy each day. This might include setting limits around the tasks that you take on at work, or choosing to prioritize important activities like sleep and self-care over other commitments.
- Who you interact with and the interactions you allow. This might mean limiting exposure to people or situations that

promote negativity and prioritizing interactions with those who bring positivity and support into your life.

- Establishing clear boundaries around what you will tolerate in your relationships and rejecting behaviors such as emotional or physical abuse, infidelity, manipulation, etc.

Reactions

Your reactions are another aspect of life that is completely in your control. Whether you choose to react with anger, frustration, or calmness in a particular situation is up to you. Your reactions may depend on the circumstances and your emotions at the time, but ultimately, the choice to express your feelings is yours.

Some potential reactions that are within your control include:

- Pausing before reacting impulsively to a stressful situation, and taking some time to reflect on your emotions to consider the best course of action.

- Communicating your feelings clearly with others, and not tolerating behaviors or actions that make you feel disrespected or mistreated.

- Focusing on positive coping strategies like breathing exercises, mindfulness practices, self-care activities like journaling or exercise, and seeking support from loved ones or a therapist when you feel overwhelmed or stressed.

While many aspects of life are out of our control, with the right approach, you can take back some power by focusing on the areas where you do have control.

Why Do Our Reactions and Behaviors Matter?

Our reactions and behaviors have a direct impact on our well-being, both mentally and physically. How we respond in a particular situation can shape the outcome and our overall sense of peace and happiness. Additionally, the way we choose to behave each day can influence how others perceive us, which can impact our relationships and professional success. By taking control of our reactions and behaviors, we can cultivate healthier habits, build stronger relationships, and feel more empowered in all areas of our lives.

What You Think and Do Is Solely up to You

Many people go through life feeling like they are on autopilot and that their reactions and behaviors are out of their control. While it's true that some circumstances are beyond our control, we always have a choice in how we respond. Our thoughts and actions are always our responsibility.

You might wonder why this is so important. After all, if we can't control what happens to us, what difference does it make how we react?

The truth is, our reactions and behaviors do matter… a lot. They impact our well-being in ways we may not even realize. For example, let's say you get cut off in traffic. Most people would respond with anger, honking their horns and flipping the other driver off. But what if, instead of getting angry, you chose to respond with compassion? You might still honk your horn to let the other driver know they made a mistake, but you do it without anger or judgment. Then you let it go and move on with your day.

Which response do you think will have a more positive impact on your day? More than likely, the compassionate response will leave you feeling calmer and less stressed than the angry response. And that's just one example.

When we react to situations with anger, frustration, or other negative emotions, it takes a toll on our physical and mental health. On the other hand, responding with positive emotions like compassion, understanding, and forgiveness can actually improve our health.

So, the next time you find yourself in a difficult situation, take a moment to pause and consider how you want to respond. Remember, you always have a choice. And what you think and do matters.

Proper Management of Life Depends Vastly on the Boundaries

Boundaries don't only deal with physical and mental limits; we also need to pay attention to other stipulations to achieve a healthy life. These include setting limits on our time and energy levels, communicating our needs clearly, choosing who and what activities we engage in, establishing clear boundaries around what we will tolerate in relationships, and responding calmly rather than impulsively to stressful situations.

Focusing on these aspects of life can help us regain some control and feel more balanced.

Completing Tasks and Being Engaged Is Important, but So Is Setting Limits

Far too often, we place importance on the wrong areas of our lives. Completing tasks, achieving goals, and being engaged in our work or other projects are important aspects of a healthy lifestyle. However, those obligations shouldn't come at the cost of our overall well-being. To achieve balance and happiness, it's crucial that we also set limits on how much time and energy we devote to these pursuits.

This might mean limiting the number of hours we work each day or saying no to opportunities that would require us to overextend ourselves. It may also involve communicating our needs clearly, establishing boundaries with loved ones and coworkers, or learning spond calmly instead of impulsively in stressful situations. By focusing on these areas of life and setting clear boundaries around them, we can achieve greater physical, emotional, and professional success.

Boundaries Help You Gain a Proper Image of the Overall Situation

Boundaries help us maintain our autonomy, but they also give us an important perspective on our situation. By setting clear limits, we gain a better understanding of what we're capable of and where our limits lie. This can help us focus on the activities that are truly important to us while also protecting against over-committing or becoming overwhelmed by new demands.

Additionally, having clear boundaries helps to build trust in our relationships, as our loved ones and colleagues will know exactly what to expect from us. Finally, setting boundaries can help us avoid becoming bogged down by stress or anxiety, allowing us to focus on the positive aspects of our lives and find happiness in the present moment.

Boundaries Provide Proper Guidelines to Follow

At the end of the day, setting boundaries is necessary to ensure our physical, emotional, and professional well-being. When we understand our wants, needs, and comfortability, we can make informed choices about how to spend our time and energy. Those boundaries also establish limits for others to follow, so we can be confident in how we interact with others or who we allow into our mental space. Whether we are trying to manage our own behavior or set expectations for others, boundaries provide the essential guidelines and rules that allow us to thrive and succeed.

Setting Goals and Maintaining Success Is Easier When We're Able to Set and Maintain Boundaries

A key factor that allows us to achieve success in any area of our lives is the ability to set goals, plan for them, and then take action. However, it's just as important to identify and create healthy boundaries around those goals. For example, if we are trying to lose weight, it's important that we establish limits around what foods and beverages we consume. We may also create a schedule for exercise and rest, or make time in our lives for socializing and relaxation.

Boundaries also allow us to protect ourselves from the negative consequences of stress and exhaustion. For example, if we are trying to meet a work deadline, it's essential to set limits on how much we work and make time for breaks or other activities that help us recharge.

Ultimately, when we can set boundaries around our goals and maintain them throughout the process, we can achieve greater levels of success in whatever we are striving for. Whether it's physical health and wellness, professional success, or meaningful relationships with family and friends, boundaries provide the crucial framework that allows us to succeed.

Boundaries Increase Self-Esteem Inside You

Boundaries build confidence. They help you feel more secure in your decisions and choices, which can then help boost your self-esteem. For example, if you can set and maintain healthy boundaries with a demanding partner or friend, you'll feel stronger and more capable of standing up for yourself. These positive feelings can then spill over into other areas of your life, making it easier to establish new boundaries or strengthen existing ones.

Boundaries Help Us Better Manage Our Emotions

When we set and maintain healthy boundaries, we are making a conscious choice to take care of ourselves. This can be especially important in situations where our emotions may be heightened or triggered in some way, such as when interacting with an overbearing parent or stressful work situation. In these moments, having strong boundaries can help us better manage our emotions and stay centered, even when things might be chaotic or challenging.

The True Potential of Setting the Right Boundaries in All Aspects of Life

Boundaries can help us develop more fulfilling relationships with others and with ourselves. By taking the time to understand our needs, feelings, and limits, we can create a solid foundation for healthy and happy interactions with others. In this way, boundaries are truly the magical key to creating positive change in our lives right away because we need to focus on ourselves before we can truly connect with others.

Overall, the benefits of setting healthy boundaries in your life are clear: They can help you feel more fulfilled, confident, and secure in yourself as an individual. At the same time, having strong boundaries is also a key part of effective conflict resolution and communication. When we are able to clearly articulate our needs and values, it becomes easier to negotiate and resolve conflicts with others. Then, by having healthy boundaries in all aspects of our lives, we can better manage our emotions and interactions with others.

Overall, some of the major benefits of setting boundaries include:

- Greater autonomy and control over your life.
- Protection from toxic or abusive relationships or situations.
- Better communication and conflict resolution skills.
- Boosted self-esteem and confidence.
- Improved emotional well-being.

- Greater ability to connect with others in meaningful ways.

Overall, setting healthy boundaries is a key component of living a happier and more fulfilling life.

How Boundaries Might Be the Only Way to Get You Out of the Hole

If you have struggled with a sense of hopelessness or depression, it may be because you have not set healthy boundaries for yourself. When we neglect to set boundaries, we can end up feeling like our needs and feelings are being ignored or dismissed. This can lead to brooding feelings of resentment or a desire to disconnect from others.

In many cases, we might not realize how important boundaries are until we find ourselves in a difficult or toxic situation. Perhaps you have been struggling at work, feeling overburdened and underappreciated by your boss and co-workers. Or maybe you are dealing with an abusive partner or relationship that leaves you feeling drained and unhappy on a regular basis.

Regardless of the specific circumstances, one fact is clear: Setting boundaries is often the most useful way to get yourself out of this hole and build a healthier and more fulfilling life. When we take the time to set firm limits and communicate them clearly, it gives us a sense of agency, control, and self-respect. This creates confidence and positivity that prompts us to move forward in our lives with purpose and confidence. Setting boundaries means we know who we are, what we like, and what we want. Understanding ourselves better can be the first step toward changing our lives.

Chapter 3:

Understanding and Pinpointing Your Triggers

Our triggers and boundaries go hand in hand—they are two integral pieces to our puzzle. In order to clearly understand our triggers, we must also be clear about what our boundaries are. Once we know what sets us off, we can work on finding healthy coping mechanisms and tools to deal with them in a constructive way.

What Are Triggers?

A trigger is anything—a person, place, thing, or situation—that sets off a negative reaction in us. It could be a situation that reminds us of a painful event from our past, or it could be a challenge that is happening in our present. Triggers can be external, like a person who is always putting us down, or they can be internal, like a thought or feeling we have about ourselves.

Sometimes we are aware of our triggers, and other times they are problems that we barely even notice. If you find yourself getting agitated for no apparent reason, maybe you were triggered, and you don't even realize it. Being aware of our triggers is crucial so that we can avoid them or at least be prepared for them when they do occur.

How Do Triggers Manifest?

Triggers can manifest in a variety of ways. For some people, their trigger might be a certain sound or scent that reminds them of a traumatic event. For others, it might be a certain type of person or situation that makes them feel uncomfortable.

Some common ways that triggers can manifest themselves include:

- feeling agitated or on edge
- feeling overwhelmed or out of control
- feeling defensive or combative
- feeling anxious or stressed
- feeling sad or depressed
- feeling disconnected or numb

Remember, everyone experiences triggers differently, so some of these symptoms may not resonate with you. Not everyone has the same triggers either—what might be a trigger for one person might not be a trigger for you. Also, our triggers can change over time. Something that didn't bother us in the past might affect us now, and vice versa. However, by keeping track of our triggers and managing them effectively, we can be more aware of their changes and our progress.

Why Is Understanding Your Triggers Important?

If you are unaware of what your triggers are, you won't be able to avoid them or prepare for them. Several tools can help you manage the symptoms or fear that may come along with facing your triggers. Without them, you might experience a lot of unnecessary stress and anxiety in your life. Secondly, if you don't have or understand the proper coping mechanisms, you might self-medicate. This can lead to unhealthy behaviors like self-harm or substance abuse. Finally, if you are not aware of your triggers, you cannot work on resolving the issues that they are pointing to. Acknowledging and accepting yourself is a major part of self-healing and setting boundaries.

How Can I Become Aware of My Triggers?

Luckily, as I mentioned above, we can become aware of our triggers and work on practicing safe techniques to manage them. First, pay attention to your body and your emotions. This technique requires you to be mindful of the present moment. If you notice you are feeling agitated or stressed for no apparent reason, chances are something has triggered you. Second, keep a journal and write down any time you think you were triggered. Include as many details as you can so that you can search for patterns. Was someone mean to you? Did you speak to a particular person? Were you involved in a project at work? Third, talk to someone you trust about your triggers. This could be a therapist, a friend, or a family member. Talking about our triggers can help us become more aware of them.

Acknowledging your triggers is the first step in managing them. Once you know what your triggers are, you can work on avoiding them or at least being prepared for them when they do occur.

How Can You Overcome Triggers?

After you become aware of your triggers, it's time to practice acceptance. Building up your self-esteem and confidence is a great place to start working on acceptance and overcoming your triggers. The more confident you are in yourself, the less likely you are to be affected by an action or situation. Second, find healthy coping mechanisms for when you are triggered. This could include activities like journaling, talking to a friend, or going for a walk. Third, work on resolving the issues that your triggers are pointing to. This might mean attending therapy or working through a trauma with a therapist.

Fourth, practice self-care. This includes being intentional about getting enough sleep, eating healthy, and exercising regularly. Taking care of yourself will help you be better equipped to deal with triggers when they occur. Lastly, set boundaries. Learn to say "no" to situations that don't serve you and to people who are not good for you. This will help to protect you from being triggered in the first place.

Triggers are a normal part of life, and everyone has them. However, you can overcome them by becoming aware of your triggers and having healthy coping mechanisms in place for when they do occur.

Triggers and Boundaries: How They Go Together

Setting boundaries when managing triggers is an important part of self-care. Boundaries help to protect us from being triggered in the first place. They also help us recover from a trigger once it has occurred.

There are two types of boundaries: Physical and emotional. Both types of boundaries are important for dealing with triggers.

Some examples of physical boundaries are the following:

- Only let people you trust into your personal space.
- Set limits on how much information you share with others.
- Not to be afraid to say "no."

Some examples of emotional boundaries are the following:

- Don't let others control your emotions.
- Don't take on other people's problems.
- Setting limits on how much you will help others.

Both types of boundaries are important for protecting us from being triggered. If you find you are constantly being triggered, it might be a good idea to look at your boundaries and see if they need to be adjusted.

How Boundaries Develop Inside a Person and How They Might Change Over Time

Several factors can influence the development and evolution of personal boundaries over time. For one, we may have certain beliefs or expectations about ourselves at a young age that carry on into adult life. These experiences with setting boundaries could then inform later choices and behaviors for setting boundaries in our relationships.

Another key factor is the types of relationships we have as we grow and change. Whether it's a childhood friendship, a romantic relationship, or a deep connection with a family member, these bonds can play an important role in how we set our own boundaries, both inside and outside ourselves.

Another way boundaries are formed is by the way others treat you and the expectations and assumptions they have of you. For instance, if you are frequently taken advantage of or treated poorly by others, you may develop negative beliefs about yourself that influence your boundaries. Or if others have overly high expectations for you, you may feel pressure to always perform at a certain level. This could create rigid and inflexible boundaries in your life.

In addition, other life events, such as major transitions or trauma, can also affect how we set boundaries. For example, a significant loss might make it more difficult to establish healthy boundaries with other people, or it may cause us to retreat inward and become more protective of ourselves.

These factors can contribute to the development and evolution of our personal boundaries over time. Therefore, it's important to be cognizant of how they might affect us as we navigate different relationships and situations. Ultimately, the key is to remain aware of our thoughts and feelings, while also keeping an open mind about how others might be impacted by our boundaries. By being mindful and intentional in how we set and maintain these boundaries, we can help foster healthier relationships with others and with ourselves.

Chapter 4:

What's Stopping You?

The key to setting good boundaries is to think more and act less. By becoming more self-aware and practicing assertiveness, you can improve your self-image. With clear, positive boundaries in place, you can enjoy greater professional success and healthier relationships both at work and at home.

Working Your Way Around the Problems and Solving Them One by One

You can use many strategies to overcome the underlying challenges that may prevent you from setting positive boundaries. Some of these strategies include improving your self-awareness, building your confidence, and working on your communication skills. Additionally, by learning to recognize your needs and limitations and setting clear expectations with others, you can develop the skills needed to overcome your challenges and establish healthy boundaries in all aspects of your life.

What Actually Prevents Most People From Setting Positive Boundaries in Life

Unfortunately, many reasons contribute to our hesitancy to develop boundaries. Most of all, though, is the lack of self-awareness. Only when we are aware of our limitations and needs can we set proper boundaries for others to respect.

Therefore, if you want to improve your image in front of others and prevent people from taking advantage of you, it's important to first gain better insight into your strengths and weaknesses. To help you become more self-aware, below are some common qualities that can also contribute to a lack of boundaries:

- **Overthinking and overanalyzing**: constantly thinking and rethinking every little decision can prevent you from taking action, which may lead to a lack of boundaries.

- **Fear of conflict or rejection**: Some people may hesitate to set limits with others because they fear others will see them as difficult, uncooperative, or uncaring. However, setting boundaries is not about imposing your will on others, but more about taking charge of your life and well-being.

- **Lack of assertiveness**: If you have trouble asserting yourself or communicating your needs to others, it may be difficult for you to set positive boundaries. However, with practice and some guidance, you can improve your communication skills and become better at setting boundaries with others.

- **Lack of self-esteem**: Low self-esteem can make some people feel they don't deserve to have their needs and opinions respected by others. However, it's important to remember that setting boundaries is not about being "selfish" or putting your desires above those of others. Instead, it simply means you're standing up for yourself and protecting your personal space from undue influence or intrusion.

- **Lack of self-confidence**: Besides lacking self-esteem, people may also struggle with a lack of confidence. Self-confidence is also crucial to building and maintaining your boundaries. Otherwise, you open yourself up to the influence of others who may not have your best interest at heart. However, by practicing assertiveness and communicating your needs in a calm and clear manner, you can improve your confidence and gain the respect of others.

As you can see, many factors can contribute to a lack of boundaries in life. However, by identifying any underlying issues and working on improving your self-awareness, you can learn to set positive boundaries for yourself and others that they will respect. In doing so, you will enjoy better relationships and more professional success in the long run.

Solving Overthinking and Overanalyzing

Overthinking is normal, but if it's preventing you from taking action and setting boundaries, it may be helpful to get help from a therapist or coach who can offer strategies and techniques for managing this tendency. To overcome overthinking, the first step is to practice acceptance and self-compassion. Generally, judgmental or critical inner voices can fuel this tendency, but self-acceptance will help you thrive along with your flaws.

You may also want to engage in reflection and mindfulness activities, such as journaling or meditation, in order to give your brain a break from over-analyzing. Additionally, setting realistic goals and focusing on the present moment instead of ruminating about the past or future can help you stay grounded and calm.

Another way to overcome overthinking is to use your mental energy on an unfamiliar task. For example, you might try channeling your thoughts and attention into a creative project or activity, such as painting, drawing, or running. Mind games like puzzles and brainteasers can also be a great way to engage your mind in something that is not overly taxing or stressful. This can help take your mind off whatever caused the overthinking. Then you have more space to calm down and reflect constructively.

Additionally, another practice is to befriend the emotions or feelings you are experiencing. This can help you better understand why certain thoughts or feelings might be present and provide an opportunity to express them in a non-judgmental way. By communicating honestly with yourself and others about your struggles and emotions, you can overcome the thought patterns that may fuel overthinking and establish healthy boundaries for yourself in the process.

Whatever strategies you choose, remember that the key to overcoming overthinking and setting positive boundaries is to be patient with yourself and compassionate in your approach.

Recognizing and Replacing the Self-Defeating Thoughts Inside You

To begin to heal or enhance our self-worth, it is important to recognize and replace the negative thoughts. These beliefs can hold us back from our desires and potential. However, when we become more mindful of self-criticism or feelings of inadequacy, we can actively work to replace these false beliefs with positive affirmations about our worth.

One common challenge many people face when trying to improve their self-worth is the tendency to be overly hard on themselves. This might manifest as a constant, critical inner voice. You may tell yourself that you are not good or smart enough. Or you may develop self-destructive behaviors, such as overworking or addictive habits.

Thought distortions like these can keep us stuck in negative cycles that prevent us from moving forward and reaching our goals. Unfortunately, many distortions can lead us to believe that we are not worthy of love or respect. These may include feelings of shame, guilt, or jealousy that can make us feel undeserving of happiness. To begin overcoming these negative thought patterns and improving your self-worth, start by checking in with yourself and becoming more aware of the inner thoughts that you have.

According to Sandra (2021), here are some common thought distortions and the strategies you can use to replace them with more positive affirmations:

- **Mind reading**: This happens when we assume we know what other people are thinking or feeling, without actually having any evidence to back it up, for example: *I just know my coworkers think I'm a pushover.* To overcome this thought distortion, try to get more information about the thoughts and feelings that you are attributing to others. For example, if you think someone else is judging or criticizing you, try asking them directly what they think instead of just assuming it based on your feelings.

- **Catastrophizing**: This distortion happens when we convince ourselves that something is much worse than it actually is, for example: *If I fail this test, it will mean that I'm not smart enough to go to college.* This thought can be harmful by making us feel defeated before we even try. To combat it, try reminding yourself that there are always other options and possibilities available to you. No matter what happens, there are likely ways for you to overcome obstacles and setbacks.

- **Filtering**: Filtering occurs when we only focus on the negative aspects of a situation, ignoring any positive or neutral elements, for example: *My boss didn't compliment my work today, so I must have done something wrong.* To challenge this thought distortion, try to remember that everyone has good and bad days, and that this may just be a bad day for your boss.

- **Emotional reasoning**: When we assume that our emotions indicate the truth and should dictate our actions or beliefs without further evidence, for example: *I feel embarrassed, so I must have done something wrong.* To combat this thought distortion, try to find objective evidence to support or refute your feelings. If you feel embarrassed, try asking a trusted friend or co-worker if they think you did something wrong, and what they would suggest instead.

- **Should statements**: When we place rigid demands on ourselves or others without considering the true cost of these demands, for example: *You should be a better listener.* Replace these thoughts with more flexible expectations or goals. Instead of demanding that others live up to your ideal, try simply suggesting that they do their best and seeing how it goes.

- **Labeling**: When we assign global labels to ourselves or others without taking the time to get specific information about the facts of a situation, for example: *I'm terrible at public speaking.* This can be damaging because it limits us from seeing ourselves accurately and prevents us from making improvements in specific areas. To combat this thought distortion, try asking yourself what specifically you did or said that was "terrible" about your public speaking. You may find that you actually did many things that were good, and can work on improving specific areas in the future.

- **Discounting positive events**: When we dismiss or devalue things that actually went well or could have been worse, for example: *Yeah, I guess I did okay on my presentation, but it wasn't perfect.* This prevents us from seeing the full range of our accomplishments and strengths, and makes it difficult to build on those elements in the future. To combat this thought distortion, try really focusing on your good qualities and achievements when you are feeling down about yourself. In particular, write them down to reinforce these positive aspects of yourself in your mind.

Unfortunately, many other thought distortions, such as fortune-telling or personalization, can also have negative effects on our moods and motivation to do what we want to accomplish. By recognizing each of these thought distortions and learning ways to challenge them as they come up, we can become better at accurately assessing situations and overcoming challenges without letting negative thinking get in the way.

When to realize that you are overthinking and need to stop: You're probably overthinking if you're worrying about things that are out of your control, reliving past mistakes, or dwelling on what could go wrong.

If you find yourself doing any of these things, take a step back and redirect your focus. Distract yourself with something positive or productive. Or simply take a few deep breaths and clear your brain.

Chapter 5:

Lacking Boundaries, the Human Worth, and Unconditional Love

Setting boundaries isn't always a simple task. We have all been through plenty of experiences that have taught us how hard it can be to set a firm boundary. The most important first step is to recognize the value of doing so. Once you're aware of why setting boundaries is vital for your well-being and happiness—that you can use boundaries to protect you from negative experiences or triggers—you can take the steps to make this a part of your everyday life. However, to achieve this, we need to understand why we might struggle to create boundaries and which challenges we may face.

Problems That You Will Face While Having No Boundaries in Life

As I mentioned, boundaries can help you in a variety of ways. As a result, a lack of boundaries can also affect you negatively. This can include feelings of stress, anxiety, overwhelm, and a lack of control over your own decisions and actions. Additionally, lacking boundaries in all areas of life can increase the risk of burnout or other mental health issues such as depression or substance abuse.

Below are a few other common symptoms that can arise from a lack of boundaries:

Always Overwhelmed

One of the most common problems that can happen when you don't have clear boundaries is feeling constantly overwhelmed. This can result from other people's demands on your time and energy. Or it may be due to ignoring your needs. Whatever the cause, if you are constantly overwhelmed by life's challenges, setting boundaries can help manage stress and other difficulties.

Problems Regarding Focus and Productivity

Another potential problem is difficulty focusing and completing tasks or projects. This may stem from a lack of clear priorities or from feelings of burnout due to overextending yourself. Additionally, constantly being distracted by others' needs and opinions can prevent you from focusing on your own goals and staying productive. By setting clear boundaries around your time, you can gain more control over your actions and priorities, which can give you a boost in productivity and overall success.

Easily Disturbed by Others' Actions

Yet another potential problem with not having boundaries is that you may be easily disturbed by the actions of others. For example, without clear boundaries, someone else might take advantage of your openness and impose their own expectations on you. You will also feel confused, since you will have no way of knowing whether your actions are in line with your needs and desires. Additionally, the ways others might react might bother you more than they should. Being concerned with the actions of others can be a sign that they're crossing a boundary, but perhaps you're unsure of which one.

Falling off Track From Your Goals

If you do not have clear boundaries set up in all areas of your life, it's difficult to stay on track with your goals and dreams. This may be because of a lack of focus or other priorities that prevent you from moving forward. Or it may be due to the feeling that you have no control over your actions and are constantly distracted by others' demands. Whatever the cause, take charge of your own development and set boundaries in order to maintain a healthy balance in each aspect of your life. In doing so, you will be more likely to achieve success and happiness on your terms.

Problems Regarding Finishing Tasks

One potential problem with not having boundaries in place is that you may struggle to complete tasks or projects. This can be because of difficulties prioritizing tasks, a lack of focus, or a feeling of being overwhelmed by the sheer amount of work you have to complete. Additionally, if others are constantly interrupting your workflow and demanding your time and attention, you may find it difficult to focus and get things done. Setting clear boundaries around your tasks and projects can help you better manage your time, prioritize your work, and stay focused on what's most important. This will ultimately improve your productivity and allow you to reach your goals faster.

In the end, setting boundaries is essential for maintaining a healthy balance in all areas of your life. Whether you are struggling with focus and productivity, easily disturbed by others' actions, or falling off track from your goals, having clear limits and guidelines can help you better manage stress and stay on track toward success.

Problems That Can Arise From Applying Boundaries

Boundaries can be difficult for us to adopt, especially if we are used to responding in certain ways. We may find ourselves feeling guilty or ashamed for saying "no" or setting limits with those around us. Additionally, there may be tension between people who have different views on what is acceptable behavior. Keep in mind that as you apply boundaries, you might receive pushback or be met with resistance. Recognize that it is natural to experience doubt or fear when we are learning how to set boundaries. Here are a few challenges you might face:

- **Problems with acceptance**: It can be difficult to accept that we cannot control how others think or feel about our boundaries. On the contrary, others might not accept our new boundaries or respect them. If this occurs, remember that your boundaries are for you and others don't agree with them. However, those are people you should limit your interaction with since they will likely continue to ignore your boundaries.

- **Problems with guilt**: When we set a boundary, we may feel guilty for saying no or setting limits. Remember that it is okay to prioritize yourself and take care of your needs first. You can be kind while still standing true to what you require and want.

- **Resistance from outsiders**: Our family or friends may not be on board with the changes we are trying to make. It can be hard to stand firm in these situations, but it's important to remember that they may not understand why we need boundaries.

- **Feeling alone**: It can be hard to feel like no one else is dealing with similar challenges as you. Many people experience similar emotions and thoughts when it comes to setting boundaries. Seek a support system or community of like-minded individuals who understand the importance of taking care of yourself and fostering healthy relationships.

- **Struggles with self-esteem and confidence**: When we set a boundary, we may be met with resistance or backlash. This can lead to feelings of shame and low self-esteem. Don't forget that you have the right to take care of yourself and that your boundaries are valid and important.

Even though there might be some challenges along the way, setting boundaries is an essential part of a healthy lifestyle. By understanding the potential challenges we might face, we can better prepare ourselves to apply healthy boundaries in our lives. Ultimately, having boundaries can lead to a more fulfilled life, as they protect us and provide us with a sense of safety and peace.

Human Worth: The Unconditional Reality

Our worth and value as human beings are not based on what we do or don't do. People will constantly try to put us down, criticize our actions, and find fault in what we say and think. This can be truly disempowering if we take it personally and allow these aggressive behaviors to affect how we see ourselves. However, when you understand that your worth as a person is not based on external factors such as these, you can find the strength to stay grounded, centered, and in control of what happens in your life.

The Basics of Human Worth

We may believe that our worth is determined by our achievements, successes, or what others think of us, but this is just one way of looking at things. In reality, we all have intrinsic value simply because we exist as human beings. Regardless of what others think or say about us, our inherent worth is a fundamental truth that can never be taken away from us.

What Is Human Worth?

To truly understand this concept, it's important to look at it from different perspectives—both internally and externally. On the external level, our worth is reflected in how we treat others and what values we hold as individuals. On an internal level, it's about recognizing that every person has inherent value simply because they are alive and capable of having thoughts, feelings, and actions. At its core, human worth is about recognizing our inherent value as individuals and respecting the intrinsic value of others.

It's about taking responsibility for our actions, standing up for what we believe in, and maintaining a positive mindset that allows us to flourish in all aspects of life. With these principles at the heart of our actions, we can set the right boundaries for ourselves and others, cultivate greater positivity in our relationships and interactions, and create more harmony in our lives.

Additionally, there is our sense of self-worth, which is closely related to our sense of human worth. It refers to the beliefs and feelings we have about ourselves, including our perception of our own value as individuals. When we have a strong sense of self-worth, we can maintain positive boundaries in all areas of our lives, from relationships and professional interactions to how we treat ourselves and others.

Ultimately, this is what true human worth is all about—recognizing that we deserve to be treated with respect and dignity, while treating others the same way. With this mindset and approach, we can set the right boundaries that allow us to flourish as individuals and create more positive, harmonious relationships with everyone around us.

The laws of our human worth are the following:

- We are all inherently valuable and deserving of respect, simply by virtue of being human.

- Our actions and behaviors reflect our sense of self-worth, and we must always strive to act with integrity and compassion in everything that we do.

- Set firm boundaries when dealing with others, both for our protection and to create a more harmonious, positive environment for everyone.

- We must always be mindful of the message that we are sending to the world through our actions, words, thoughts, and beliefs.

Overall, recognizing and affirming our human worth is one of the most empowering things we can do as individuals. When we truly understand that our value is not dependent on external factors, we can take control of our lives and create more positive, fulfilling relationships with those around us. We have the power to shape the world in which we live; by acknowledging our worth and treating others with compassion and respect, we can help cultivate a better future for all.

Unconditional Love

Unconditional human worth is the understanding that every person is worthy of love and respect, regardless of their circumstances or achievements. This concept can be especially challenging for people who struggle with negative thoughts and emotions. These feelings often lead to self-criticism and blame when we encounter losses or disappointments.

However, by accepting our core worth and embracing it as truth, we can break out of negative thought patterns. This can help us stay grounded, resilient, and focused as we navigate the challenges that inevitably arise throughout our lives.

What Unconditional Love Can Give You

Unconditional love is a powerful force that can help you overcome negative thoughts and emotions and stay focused on what really matters to you. Whether this comes from your family, friends, or loved ones, unconditional love provides the support and comfort you need to move forward in life with gratitude and optimism. Additionally, practicing self-love through affirming positive thoughts can also help you overcome negative thinking patterns and give you the perspective and resilience that you need to stay focused on your goals.

Understanding the Language of Love

Besides affirming thoughts and cultivating positive emotions, it is also important to learn the language of love. The language of love is essential for building strong relationships, as it helps you express your feelings and needs in a clear and authentic way. This can include communicating about your emotions and desires in a positive way, setting boundaries when needed, or simply expressing that you are grateful for someone's presence in your life. By learning to speak the language of love, you can create more meaningful relationships, make it easier to meet your needs in a healthy way, and enjoy greater happiness and satisfaction in the present moment.

Appreciating the Opinion of Others

Other people's opinions are not a reflection of your self-worth. While it can be hard not to take criticism or negative feedback personally, everyone has different perspectives and experiences, so what others may see as flaws in you may actually be strengths or skills. On the contrary, their negative comments could have some weight, and simply giving them a little more consideration can help you grow as a person.

Additionally, if someone offers you praise or encouragement, try to accept it graciously and let their words resonate with you. By respecting the opinions of others and accepting their kind words as valid and true, you can cultivate a deeper sense of inner strength and confidence in yourself, even when things don't go your way. Whether you are struggling with self-criticism or feeling discouraged by setbacks, embracing your worth as a human being can help you feel more confident and resilient, regardless of what comes your way.

Accepting and Acknowledging Positive Qualities

You might believe you're full of flaws, but that doesn't mean you should neglect your positive qualities. It's hard to accept compliments or acknowledge your strengths, but doing so is an important part of building self-confidence.

To start, try taking a moment each day to reflect on the things that make you unique, such as your strengths and abilities. Acknowledging and embracing your positive qualities can also help you build resilience when times get tough. By focusing on what is going well in your life and appreciating all that you have to be grateful for, you can learn to reframe negative situations or thoughts in a more positive light. By practicing self-compassion and extending kindness towards yourself, you can be more fully present in your life and focus on what truly matters.

Cultivate Body Appreciation and Acceptance

Some power comes from knowing your worth is not measured by your physical appearance. In a society that often places a high value on looks and attractiveness, it's easy to fall into the trap of focusing on what you perceive as "flaws" or areas of your body that you dislike. However, engaging in self-criticism or comparing yourself to others can leave you feeling down on yourself and diminish your sense of self-worth.

One powerful way to boost your body's appreciation and acceptance is to practice self-compassion by treating yourself with kindness and understanding. This tenderness applies at all times, even if you don't believe you meet a certain beauty ideal. This might involve taking the time to do things you enjoy, such as going for a walk in nature or treating yourself to a bubble bath. Focusing on the positive aspects of your appearance can also help you cultivate more body appreciation and self-love. Whether it's noticing how strong your legs are when running or appreciating the curves of your lips and eyes, acknowledging what makes you unique can help you feel more content in your skin.

Assert Self-Love and Appreciation

A strong sense of self-worth can also help you feel more confident in your relationships and communicate honestly and openly with others. Self-love can be as simple as treating yourself with kindness and respect, or as bold as speaking up for what you need. Asserting your self-love and appreciation can help you feel more grounded in your relationships and establish healthy boundaries that reflect what matters most to you. It improves your self-worth, which allows you to connect more deeply with others and create healthy relationships that are based on mutual respect, understanding, and compassion. At the end of the day, cultivating self-love and appreciation is an important way to come into your power as a unique and complete human being.

Overcoming These Challenges

Acknowledge and Accept Reality the Way That It Is

Have you ever been so upset that you felt like every part of your life was going wrong? For example, maybe someone in your life told you they would rather not be friends anymore or a project at work went completely off the rails. Feeling good about yourself and moving forward when these kinds of situations happen might seem impossible. However, even in these situations, it's essential to acknowledge and accept reality as it is.

Radical acceptance is a cognitive-behavioral therapy (CBT) technique developed by Dr. Marsha Linehan. This technique involves recognizing that any situation is what it is, even if you don't like it or agree with it. Essentially, this means that you actively accept the reality of your current situation, even if it feels unpleasant or upsetting.

Radical acceptance is ultimately about acknowledging who you are as a person or how a situation affects you and being okay with it. You acknowledge and accept yourself and your experiences in a non-judgmental way. There might be room for improvements, and we're willing to work towards them with an open and loving mind. This technique is something we do for ourselves, rather than trying to convince others to see life how we do. It can help you move past upsetting thoughts and emotions to focus on what you need and want in the present moment.

That means accepting who you are, what you have, and what has happened in your life in a realistic, non-judgmental way. This can be particularly challenging if you are prone to negative thinking patterns or other thought distortions like those described above, but it's the ultimate tool for self-improvement.

Understand Your Core Worth

In order to overcome negative thoughts and emotions, start by embracing your core worth. This means understanding that you are worthy of love and respect, just as you are. As I mentioned above, our humanity and self-worth are independent of our achievements and failures. Understanding this is crucial—accept it as truth, and internalize these ideas so that they become a natural part of how you think and behave.

Often, people who struggle with negative thoughts and emotions tend to engage in self-criticism or blame when things don't go the way they want them to or when they experience losses and disappointments. With the art of recognizing your core worth and learning to embrace it, you can break out of these negative thought patterns. Instead of assuming the worst about yourself or others, you can begin focusing on what matters most to you at any moment, without letting negative thoughts get in the way.

Create the Habit of Affirming Thoughts

Besides accepting the reality of the situation that you are in, it's helpful to create a habit of affirming thoughts that are positive and helpful. Since thought distortions are essentially unhelpful patterns of thinking that skew your perception of reality, it is important to develop the habit of affirming thoughts that are actually helpful in a situation. For example, if you have just received some difficult or unpleasant news and fall into ruminative thought patterns about how unfair life is, stop for a moment. Think about a few positive thoughts that you can tell yourself in this situation.

This might include reminding yourself that you are loved and supported by the people around you, or that everything will work out for the best. By creating a habit of affirming positive thoughts when you need them most, you can override negative thinking patterns. This allows you to focus, so you can gain some perspective in difficult times and stay focused on what matters most. If you are struggling with negative thoughts or emotions, reframing your thoughts to be more affirming can be a powerful tool to help you overcome these challenges. By understanding your core worth and creating the habit of affirming helpful thoughts, you can take control of your thinking patterns and begin to reach your goals in a more stable and focused way.

Chapter 6:

How Boundaries and the Necessary Skills Can Ease Personal Growth

Setting boundaries in your personal life can be challenging, especially if you know what it's like to let others walk all over you or if saying "no" troubles you. But let me tell you this: You are not alone. Many people have experienced the difficulties of setting boundaries in their personal lives, and with the right tools and strategies, it can be much easier than you think.

Understanding the Importance of Having Boundaries in Each Sector of Life

Boundaries are not only for setting limits with people you are close to; they can help you set limits in all areas of your life, including work, relationships, self-care, and more. By establishing clear boundaries for yourself, you are taking control over your well-being and giving yourself the power to make decisions that are in line with your values and goals.

The Harsh Result of Allowing Others to Trample Your Boundaries

When boundaries are not set, we tend to allow other people to take advantage of us. This may occur in relationships, work environments, or any other situation that involves interaction with others. For instance, we may be afraid to speak up when we feel wronged or disrespected, or we may be too accommodating in our relationships. Without proper boundaries, people around us can start taking advantage of our kindness and generosity.

The result is often feeling taken advantage of, used, and unappreciated. By undergoing boundary-setting exercises and properly communicating our needs to those around us, we can prevent ourselves from falling victim to unfair expectations. Boundaries help us realize where our limits are, but they can also stop you from immediately reacting or overreacting when faced with a challenging situation. Setting boundaries is an important step to creating a life of peace and balance. It allows us to be our true selves, form healthy relationships, and create meaningful connections with those around us. It creates and maintains the calmness within.

Why Are Boundaries Important?

There are many benefits to having healthy boundaries. When we set boundaries, we are taking care of ourselves and our needs. This helps us to feel good about ourselves and to be more effective in our relationships with others. Setting boundaries can also

- reduce stress and anxiety.
- improve communication.
- build trust.
- promote respect.
- foster healthy relationships.

Setting Boundaries and the Different Types

Now that we understand what boundaries are and why they are important, let's explore the different boundaries you need to understand and apply.

How to Set Boundaries

For starters, it's important to recognize what your boundaries are. This can include physical and emotional limitations that you impose on yourself. Once you have identified these boundaries, it is time for you to communicate them to those around you in a loving and respectful manner. Doing so is an essential part of protecting and taking care of yourself. Communicate effectively and practice being assertive by clearly and gently expressing your needs, wants, and desires.

Additionally, it's important to be aware of the boundaries of those around you. When engaging with others, remember to respect their boundaries as well and avoid making assumptions about what they are comfortable with or interested in.

Another important step in setting boundaries is to learn how to say "no." This means not only saying "no" when necessary but also being firm and standing by your decision, no matter how much opposition you may face from others. This doesn't necessarily mean being selfish or unkind. It simply means that you are taking control of your wellbeing and making decisions to protect yourself.

Additionally, ensure that your boundaries are respected by the people around you. If someone crosses one of your defined boundaries, it's important to assertively communicate this to them and make sure they understand why their behavior is not acceptable.

By setting and following boundaries, we can protect ourselves from those who may take advantage of our kindness. We can also foster healthy relationships with others and create meaningful connections that are based on mutual respect. Boundaries are essential to a peaceful life and should be adopted by everyone for their safety and well-being.

Different Types of Boundaries That You Need to Understand and Apply

Here are the different types of boundaries that you need to understand and apply:

Time Boundaries

Time boundaries are the limits we set on how much time we spend with others. They can also be related to the amount of time we spend on certain activities. For example, you may need to set a boundary with a friend who always wants to talk on the phone for hours at a time. You may also need to create your own limits if you find you are spending too much time on social media or focusing on the wrong projects. If you're a workaholic, you may want to set boundaries about how much time you spend at the office and how much work you're willing to take home.

Communication Boundaries

Communication boundaries are the limits we set on how and when we communicate with others. They can be related to the content of our communication, as well as the frequency and medium. For instance, maybe you can set boundaries around late night text messaging. You may also need to determine which limits to set if you find yourself intruding on others' communication boundaries, especially late at night or when you should focus on an important task. This can also include how you allow others to speak to you or what type of language you tolerate. Maybe you're uncomfortable with swearing or graphic jokes—this would be a boundary.

Setting Boundaries on Defensiveness

Defensiveness is a natural reaction to feeling threatened or attacked. When we feel defensive, we are more likely to lash out at others or withdraw into ourselves. If you find you are frequently feeling defensive, it may be time to set some boundaries around how you react to and communicate with others. For example, maybe you can choose to not react to criticism until you have calmed down and thought about it logically. You may also need to establish limits with a friend or family member who is always putting you down.

Setting Boundaries on Energy Vampires

Energy vampires are people who drain us emotionally and mentally. They may be negative, critical, or just plain exhausting to be around. If you frequently feel drained after spending time with someone, it may be time to set a boundary around how much time you spend with them or how you interact with them. These boundaries might include saying no to requests for your time or energy, setting limits on how much you will help them, and taking breaks from activities that leave you feeling drained.

Boundary Violations

Sometimes people may violate our boundaries, even if they don't mean to. For example, a friend may show up at your house without calling first, or a family member may start talking about a sensitive topic before you're ready to discuss it. If someone violates your boundaries, it's important to communicate with them about it. Let them know what boundary they violated and why it was important to you. This will help them understand your needs and hopefully prevent them from violating your boundaries in the future.

Anger Boundaries

A crucial limitation we can set is an anger boundary. This boundary controls and enforces how much anger we will allow ourselves to feel or express. This boundary is necessary because anger is a powerful emotion that can easily get out of control. When we are angry, we are more likely to say or do things that we later regret. If you're resentful or angry often, it may be time to set a boundary. Instead of reeling in anger, walk away from an argument or stop speaking to someone who consistently makes you angry.

Boundaries in Social Communications

In our fast-paced, constantly connected world, setting boundaries around our social media use is more necessary than ever. Otherwise, we can easily spend too much time on our phones and computers and not enough time interacting with the people around us. Unfortunately, social media was specifically designed to capture and maintain our attention, so we might feel like the odds are against us when setting boundaries.

However, this boundary, like many others, requires you to be intentional. For example, set a rule that you will only check your phone once an hour or that you will not use social media after 9 p.m. Use an app to limit your access or turn your phone off completely. Don't let the phone charge next to your bed. Additionally, you may need to be strict about who you allow on your feed. The more negative people you allow in your life, the more likely you are to feel shamed or struggle with your goals and boundaries. So, consider setting a boundary that you will only follow people who make you feel good about yourself or your life.

Boundaries in Friendships

Friendship is a crucial, but often one of the toughest, area to set limitations. Friendships are supposed to be based on mutual respect and understanding. However, sometimes they can become one-sided or even toxic. If you're in a friendship that is no longer healthy or isn't equal, it may be time to set a boundary. Consider setting limits with a friend who is always negative or critical. Or you may want to establish how you will allow your friends to speak to you. This might involve spending less time with this friend or no longer sharing personal information with them.

Boundaries in Intimacy

When it comes to setting boundaries in intimacy, it's important to remember that you have the right to say no at any time, for any reason. Intimacy can mean different things to different people. For example, some people may feel comfortable kissing on the first date, while others may not. The same could be true for a greeting hug. There is no right or wrong answer; it's simply important to make sure that you are only doing what you are comfortable with and that the other person is respecting your wishes. If you find yourself in a situation where you feel pressured to do something you don't want to, then don't do it.

Boundaries With Gossip

Gossip can be harmful and hurtful, so it's important to set boundaries around it. For example, you might want to limit hanging out with people who like to gossip. This can be difficult if you find yourself in a social setting where everyone is talking about each other, but it's important to remember that you don't have to participate if you don't want to. You may also need to set a boundary with someone who is always gossiping about you. This might include walking away from the conversation or telling the person you don't want to hear gossip.

Sexual Boundaries

Sexual boundaries are important to set in order to ensure that you are only engaging in activities that you are comfortable with. For example, you may want to set a boundary that you will not have sex without a condom. You may also decide that you will not have sex until you are ready to make the commitment. Sex is a normal and wonderful part of life, but you should be comfortable and confident when taking that step in a relationship. Also remember, just because you said yes one time doesn't mean that the person has an all-access-pass to your body.

You can change your mind at any time, and they should respect that decision.

Gender Boundaries

Gender boundaries are important to set to ensure that you are only doing what you feel comfortable with. For example, you may refrain from wearing revealing clothing if it makes you feel uncomfortable. You may also choose not to engage in any physical activity that makes you feel uncomfortable. Additionally, if you identify with a different gender than what was assigned to you at birth, it's important to set boundaries around how you want to be referred to and what pronouns you use. Keep in mind that not everybody is going to understand or even be aware of your gender identity, so it's important to be patient and educate them in a way that feels comfortable for both of you.

Possession and Spiritual Boundaries

You may feel comfortable sharing your possessions with others, but there are also times when you need to set a boundary around them. For example, maybe you decide not to lend money to friends or family members, so you can avoid feelings of obligation and resentment if the debt is not repaid.

Additionally, if you're spiritual or religious, set boundaries around how you practice your faith. For example, maybe you refrain from participating in certain religious rituals if they make you feel uncomfortable, or you may establish boundaries about what you're willing to communicate with others or what comments you're willing to accept. Practicing your faith in a way that feels authentic and true for you is an important part of connecting with yourself.

The bottom line is that we all have different comfort levels with setting boundaries. It's important to be aware of your limits and to communicate them to others. Additionally, it's important to respect the boundaries of others, even if you don't agree with them. We all have the right to set boundaries that work for us and our relationships.

Understanding the Importance of Now and Acting Quickly to Bring Positive Change in Your Life

Our minds are always active, and they have the tendency to wander towards chaos. To combat this, practicing present moment awareness is critical in terms of rebuilding self-confidence and self-esteem. This means acknowledging and observing your thoughts, feelings, sensations, and the surrounding environment without judgment or criticism. By doing so, you will be better able to move beyond negative thinking patterns that can damage your confidence and focus on what is happening right now.

By focusing on the present, you can also challenge yourself and push your limits. This may involve setting new goals, taking on new challenges, or simply stepping out of your comfort zone in small ways every day. This helps you build resilience and trust in yourself, and it can also lead to a more positive outlook on life.

Acting quickly is also important, as procrastination can be a major barrier to achieving your goals. Luckily, by embracing the present moment, you will be better able to focus your energy and attention on moving forward towards what you want in life. This will minimize stress, worry, and other negative emotions. One effective way to do this is through mindfulness practices such as meditation or deep breathing exercises. These techniques prompt you to focus on an activity, an object, or only your breath to clear your mind so you can be present.

Now that we understand the importance of boundaries, in the following chapters, we will explore some key boundaries for various areas of your life. By understanding the importance of now and taking action towards these goals, you can begin to reclaim your self-confidence and transform your life for the better.

Chapter 7:

Boundaries to Consider for a Peaceful Life

In this chapter, we will explore how to set healthy boundaries in life and in love. As we have learned in previous chapters, our self-esteem is key to our ability to set boundaries. When we have healthy self-esteem, we are more likely to set boundaries that are respectful and beneficial to both ourselves and others.

Some people prefer to set strict boundaries, while others prefer to be more flexible. Your personal circumstances are also crucial when setting boundaries. For example, if you have a history of being treated poorly by others, set stricter boundaries than someone who has not had such experiences. If you're not sure where to start, luckily, this chapter reviews the different boundaries to consider setting in your life.

Understanding When and Where to Draw the Line

Understanding your limitations is essential for maintaining healthy relationships with others. You need to communicate your boundaries to others clearly and assertively, which means you have to understand what you're asking for. Here are some signs that you may need to implement a boundary or more boundaries in your life:

- You frequently say "yes" to things that you really don't want to do.

- You have a hard time saying "no" to others.
- You allow others to take advantage of you.
- You often feel used by others.
- You have difficulty sticking up for yourself.
- You find yourself in harmful or abusive situations.
- You experience mood swings related to stress.
- You frequently feel anxious or angry.

If any of these sound familiar, it may be time to start setting some boundaries. Pinpoint the situation or person that elicited that response and determine which limits to set. Keep in mind that there is no one-size-fits-all solution—the type and severity of boundary you need will vary depending on your individual circumstances.

How Much Are You Willing to Let Yourself off the Track?

When you set boundaries, determine how flexible you are with each one. For example, if developing more healthy habits is important to you, are you willing to let yourself get off track with your diet or fitness routine? If so, how often and by how much? Will you allow constructive comments? If so, from whom, and how often? Where does your threshold for criticism or distractions come into play?

By being realistic with your boundaries, you can ensure that you can stick to them. If you're not realistic, you may constantly break your own boundaries, which can lead to feelings of guilt or shame.

Don't forget to consider the consequences of breaking your own boundaries. For example, if you break your diet boundary, you may feel guilty or ashamed. If you break your fitness boundary, you may miss out on the benefits of exercise. How would you react in this situation?

How do you break out of the cycle? What techniques can you implement? If you break your boundary around constructive comments, you may allow someone to hurt your feelings. As a result, determine if you will bend your rules, how much so, and under what circumstances.

Boundaries protect your physical, emotional, and mental health. You can feel more confident in saying no to a person or an activity that you don't want to do. You will establish healthy relationships and maintain a sense of self. Keep in mind that setting boundaries is a process, and it may take some time to figure out what works for you. However, with healthy and proper boundaries in place, you can find peace in your life.

The Importance of Having Peace and the Correlation With Self-Esteem

When you have peace in your life, it means that you're not constantly feeling anxious, stressed, or overwhelmed. You're able to take a step back and relax. This can be difficult to do if you don't have healthy boundaries in place.

For example, if you don't have a boundary around your time, you may say "yes" to a party you don't want to go to. Or attending a gathering that is not in your best interest. When you accomplish a task to appease others, you can harbor feelings of resentment. You may question who has control of your life. However, with proper boundaries, you're able to say "no" to an offer that doesn't serve you, which helps you find peace.

A strong correlation exists between having peace in your life and having high self-esteem. When you have more self-esteem, you have more peace because you are confident in your decisions. As your life becomes more peaceful, your self-esteem increases tenfold. This allows you to nurture your relationships and yourself in a supportive and beneficial way. As a result, you're able to feel good about yourself and your life.

Why Treating the Mind Properly Is as Important as Treating the Body Properly

Treat your mind with the same respect that you would treat your body. Our minds are just as important as our bodies, and we need to take care of them both. Our minds, unlike our bodies, are constantly thinking, processing, and creating. Even as we sleep, our brains don't take a break. Therefore, if we don't take care of our minds, it can lead to feelings of anxiety, stress, and overwhelm.

However, the opposite occurs. Far too often, we focus more on our bodies—ensuring we eat a well-rounded diet or drink eight glasses of water a day. However, we forget to treat our minds with the same care. We need to ensure we're getting enough sleep, taking breaks throughout the day, and spending time doing activities we enjoy. When we take care of our minds, we find peace in our lives.

This means that we should set boundaries around our thoughts and emotions, just as we would set limits around our physical space and time. For example, if you're engaging in negative self-talk, establish strict boundaries about how you speak to yourself. Or, if you often compare yourself to others, determine what triggers those thoughts, and set boundaries appropriately.

Understanding What You Truly Need

Understanding what you truly need draws the connection between your behavior. When you're aware of what you want, you can understand why you're acting a certain way and try a different communication method. To do this, you have to understand your wants and needs. "Wants" can be anything that is nice to have, but not essential. For example, you may want a new car but not need one. On the contrary, needs are things that are essential for your survival or well-being. For example, you need food, water, and shelter. Additionally, our needs correlate to our boundaries.

For example, you may need space and alone time in order to feel relaxed and at peace. Or, set a boundary around how much time you spend with other people in order to avoid feeling overwhelmed. When you understand your needs, it can help you find peace in your life.

Identifying Your Core Values

Your core values are at the heart of why you are you. Core values are the qualities that are most important to you. They're the foundation of who you are, and they guide your decision-making. When you know your core values, you're able to make choices that align with your beliefs.

For example, if one of your core values is family, you may choose to spend more time with your loved ones, even if it means sacrificing in other areas of your life. Or, if one of your core values is adventure, you may choose to take a trip to an exotic country, even if it's outside of your comfort zone. When you make choices that align with your core values, you'll be happy, confident, or excited, even if it's scary.

Additionally, a lack of boundaries can affect your relationship with others. You may not nurture your relationships appropriately. For example, if you don't set boundaries around your time, you may never have any time for yourself. Or, if you're constantly giving to others without taking care of yourself, it can lead to resentment.

Doing Versus Overdoing

The distinction between doing and overdoing is crucial for setting boundaries because we don't want to completely isolate ourselves, even if it feels good. Doing is taking action in a healthy and controlled manner. For example, if you're feeling overwhelmed, you may take some time for yourself in order to relax and recharge. Or, if you're feeling angry, you may express your anger constructively. On the contrary, overdoing is taking action in a way that is harmful and destructive. For example, if you're feeling overwhelmed, you may be numbing yourself with drugs or alcohol. Or, if you're feeling angry, you may lash out at others in a destructive way.

In the end, "doing" leads to peace, while "overdoing" leads to chaos. When you're able to find the balance between doing and overdoing, you're more likely to find peace in your life.

What Happens When You Set Boundaries That Are Too Strict

Unfortunately, sometimes we can go from one extreme to the next: No boundaries to having way too many boundaries. This usually happens when we've been hurt in the past, and we become afraid of getting hurt again. As a result, we build up walls around us to protect ourselves.

However, setting boundaries that are too strict can actually be harmful. Setting too many boundaries can cause us to not interact with others or make us want to stay home and avoid people.

Additionally, setting boundaries that are too strict can affect your relationship with others. For example, if your boundaries are too strict around time, you may have no time for others. Or, if you don't connect with others because you don't allow yourself to open up or engage in activities that let you get to know others.

While setting boundaries is healthy and can help you find peace in your life, it's important to find a balance. This means setting boundaries that are neither too lax nor too strict. When you're able to find the balance, you're more likely to find peace in your life.

If you set boundaries that are too strict, it can lead to isolation and loneliness. However, you're only avoiding being open and vulnerable with others. Or, the lack of balance can make you feel like you're not living a fulfilling life.

Boundaries Help You Identify Yourself

When determining which boundaries to set, it can help you understand who you are and what you want in life. Setting boundaries requires you to make choices about your time, emotions, and thoughts—and they have to support you positively; otherwise, it can lead to chaos. It requires you to understand yourself, your triggers, wants, and needs.

Creates a Zone for Yourself

When you set boundaries, it can help you create a "zone" for yourself. Boundaries are like a fence. Your body and mind are the house, and the fence is the boundary. The fence protects your house from burglars and intruders. In the same way, boundaries shelter you from people and situations that are harmful or toxic. Just like a fence, you can always open the gate and let people in, but you can also close the gate and keep people out. We all have a need for boundaries because they provide us with a sense of safety and security.

You Can Understand What You Are Capable of and What You Are Willing to Do Even Better

Boundaries can help you understand your capabilities and limits. You need to know yourself well, because if you don't, then you'll set the wrong boundaries and may feel overwhelmed or taken advantage of. However, when you understand your abilities and capabilities, you're more likely to set the right and healthy boundaries for your needs. As a result, you'll feel more in control of your life and less stressed.

Additionally, this internal inventory allows you to pinpoint the areas in your life that could use more work. This can be anything from taking on a new hobby to communicating better with your family. Once you've identified the areas that need work, you can create boundaries around these areas in order to protect yourself from stress and anxiety.

Or you can improve some of your qualities so you can enhance your relationships with others.

Chapter 8:

Eight Most Important Tactics to Improve Your Self-Esteem

How to improve your self-esteem is a very important question for many people. In order to set and maintain boundaries, you must have good self-esteem because this allows you to believe in yourself and what you are doing. In this chapter, we will review the eight most important tactics to improve your self-esteem.

Write Down What You Admire About Yourself

By recognizing and focusing on your positive qualities, you can begin to see yourself in a more positive light. This can also help you challenge any negative or self-critical thoughts that you may have about yourself.

- **Keep a journal**: Start by writing down a list of your positive qualities, such as your intelligence, creativity, compassion, or kindness. You can also write about specific things that you have accomplished or challenges that you have overcome.

- **Reflect on your accomplishments**: Spend some time each day reflecting on the things that you are proud of. This could be something as simple as finishing a project at work or helping someone in need.

- **Practice acceptance**: Humans are not perfect, and you don't need to be perfect in order to have good self-esteem. Accept yourself just as you are, flaws and all, and work on accepting other people as well.

- **Use affirmations**: By focusing on the positive things in your life, you can begin to feel more grateful and happy. Consider using affirmations to help reinforce these positive feelings, such as *I am enough,* or *I accept myself just as I am.*

Avoid the Tendency to Please Others All the Time

Many people with low self-esteem tend to put the needs and desires of other people ahead of their own. While this can be beneficial in some situations, it can often leave you feeling drained and unhappy. When you avoid pleasing others, you:

- **feel less overwhelmed**: By focusing on your needs and desires first, you can avoid feeling overextended or burned out. This allows you to take better care of yourself and set healthy boundaries with others.

- **can manage your expectations**: When you stop putting so much pressure on yourself to please others, you can better manage your expectations. This prompts you to be more realistic about what you are capable of.

- **set and achieve life goals easier**: Focusing on your needs can also help you achieve your goals and set boundaries for yourself. This allows you to concentrate on what is important and focus on making progress, rather than worrying about how others perceive you.

Step Outside Your Comfort Zone

For many people with low self-esteem, pushing yourself out of your comfort zone can be anxiety-provoking and uncomfortable. But trying new activities and facing your fears can help you boost your self-confidence and improve your self-image.

When taking on new challenges, some strategies that you can try include: Setting small, manageable goals for yourself; seeking out positive role models; and reaching out to others for support when you need it.

Ultimately, stepping out of your comfort zone helps you reach new heights of capability and confidence. By pushing yourself, you can gain a greater sense of self-worth and feel more empowered, which will help you build better boundaries with others.

Comparisons and What to Do With It

Comparing yourself with other people is a common habit for many individuals, particularly those with low self-esteem. Focusing on what others are doing or the luxuries that they have—and feeling like you don't measure up in comparison—is an easy but hurtful cycle to end up in. However, comparisons can be unhealthy if we let them consume us and make us doubt our worth and abilities.

The goal with this step is to find a healthy balance. Comparisons that let you down should be avoided. For instance, focusing on a friend's successes and comparing yourself to them may leave you feeling inadequate. At the same time, don't be afraid to seek inspiration from others. Engaging with people who are doing well in areas where you struggle can motivate you to achieve your goals and improve yourself.

What Are Healthy Comparisons?

Healthy comparisons are those that inspire you to reach your full potential without causing you to feel inadequate or lacking. For example, comparing yourself to a classmate who is excelling in school can be motivating, as it encourages you to work harder and achieve better grades. It could even be a friendly face-off, with both people pushing the other to strive higher. However, the most significant difference between a healthy and unhealthy comparison is how you internalize the information.

If you allow comparisons to consume you and make you feel bad about yourself, then they are probably not healthy for you. If you can reframe that thought to push you to accomplish your goals and become the best version of yourself, then they are a valuable tool.

Some tips for comparison include:

- Setting realistic expectations for your performance.

- Focusing on your strengths and what you can do rather than focusing on other people's achievements.

- Seeking out supportive friends and mentors who can help you stay focused on your own progress.

With these strategies, you can use comparison as a tool to achieve your goals and improve yourself while minimizing the negative impact it might otherwise have on your self-esteem.

Overall, be mindful of how you engage in comparisons and make sure that they are constructive and help you grow rather than hold you back. With these strategies in place, you can regain a positive perspective on your life and build better boundaries with others.

Forgive Yourself for the Past Negative Thoughts

Often, individuals with low self-worth tend to dwell on past mistakes and feel guilty and ashamed about their actions. However, carrying a sense of guilt and shame can be detrimental to your mental health and prevent you from moving forward with your life.

To improve your self-esteem, it's important to learn to forgive yourself for past mistakes and focus on the present instead.

One strategy that can help is to practice self-compassion. This means acknowledging your humanity and accepting that you are imperfect, just like everyone else. Rather than dwelling on negative thoughts or beating yourself up over small missteps, reflect on the mistakes you have made. Practice forgiving yourself for mishaps. This will help you refocus your energy on what's important and move forward with a positive mindset.

Other tips for forgiving yourself include setting realistic expectations, focusing on the present rather than the past, and seeking supportive friends or mentors who can offer support as you work through this process. With these strategies in mind, you can learn to let go of guilt and shame from the past and embrace your present self with confidence and optimism.

Set Boundaries in Your Relationships

Setting boundaries and self-esteem go hand-in-hand. They grow stronger together. When you set firm boundaries and stand confident in your decisions, you develop your self-worth and increase your esteem.

Some strategies to help improve your boundaries include being assertive, setting clear limits, speaking up for yourself, and sticking to your decisions. Additionally, it can be helpful to practice healthy communication skills and actively listen to what others have to say. If you find that certain relationships or situations are difficult to navigate or make you feel uncomfortable, it may be wise to consider removing yourself from those situations.

Celebrating Wins (Even the Smallest Ones)

When we celebrate our wins, we release dopamine, which then helps us feel motivated, focused, and confident. Reaching our milestones can be a great way to boost our self-esteem and give ourselves the motivation we need to continue on.

To celebrate your wins, try setting small goals for yourself that are realistic and attainable. Then, when you achieve those goals, allow yourself to reward yourself in some way. You can do this by setting aside time for yourself, doing something nice for your body, or practicing other self-care strategies that make you feel good. Maybe you can take yourself to the movies or go out to dinner with friends. Whatever it is, be sure to savor the moment and enjoy your experience. Don't forget—even the smallest wins deserve to be celebrated, as they help to reinforce positive behaviors and keep you moving forward in a healthy way.

Simply recognizing and acknowledging your accomplishments can help you feel confident, motivated, and proud of yourself.

Let Go of Negative People and Toxic Relationships

When you are struggling with low self-esteem, it can be tempting to latch onto relationships that feed your insecurities. However, these types of negative relationships can have a detrimental effect on your mental health, and they may even cause you to feel worse about yourself over time.

To let go of negative people or toxic relationships, start by identifying who or what these people are in your life. Consider if this relationship is healthy and supportive, or if it may actually be causing more harm than good in your life. Then, think about how you can begin to remove yourself from that situation or relationship.

Some strategies that can help include setting boundaries with the person, focusing on the positive aspects of your relationship (if any), and thinking about ways that you can improve your self-esteem without relying on others. And remember—while it may be difficult to let go of these relationships initially, over time you will find new support systems in place. As you surround yourself with positive and supportive people, you will begin to feel happier and more confident in yourself.

Whether it's a friend, family member, or co-worker, be mindful of the relationships in your life and how they may affect your self-esteem. By focusing on setting boundaries and letting go of toxic relationships, you can begin to feel more confident, motivated, and proud of yourself.

Ultimately, improving your self-esteem takes time and patience. By taking these steps, you can set healthy boundaries in your relationships and develop a stronger sense of yourself. With confidence and resilience, you can embrace who you are and become the best version of yourself.

So, if you're struggling with boundaries and self-esteem, remember that it's never too late to take steps towards improving both.

Chapter 9:

Developing Self-Confidence

As I briefly discussed in the previous chapters, your self-confidence and self-esteem will always play a role in the way you feel about yourself and the way you operate in your everyday life. Your level of self-confidence will affect your ability to set boundaries. If you have low self-confidence, you may find it more difficult to set boundaries because you don't believe in your own values.

You may also find it difficult to say "no" or to assert yourself. On the other hand, if you have high self-confidence, you're more likely to set boundaries because you believe in your value, and you know how to assert yourself. Luckily, you can increase your self-confidence with a few techniques, and that's what we'll review in this chapter.

Understanding Self-Confidence

The best and most natural self-confidence doesn't come from what you own, who you know, or what you've accomplished. It comes from within. When you have inner confidence, you are secure in yourself and your abilities, regardless of what is happening around you. Inner confidence is unshakable and allows you to approach life with a positive attitude, no matter what challenges you face.

Developing inner confidence requires that you first get to know and accept yourself. This means taking the time to understand your values, your strengths, and your weaknesses. Once you have a good understanding of who you are, it becomes much easier to be confident in yourself. In this chapter, we'll review how to cultivate more self-confidence from within.

Self-confidence is the belief that you can accomplish a goal or handle a situation effectively. You have trust and faith in your own abilities and capabilities. When you have self-confidence, you feel secure and certain about yourself. You know your strengths and weaknesses, and you accept them. You also believe in your ability to overcome challenges and grow as a person. Self-confidence differs from self-esteem. Self-esteem is about how much you like, respect, and approve of yourself.

Self-esteem is about how much value you place on yourself. When you have high self-esteem, you have a positive opinion of yourself. You see yourself as a deserving person. On the contrary, when you have low self-esteem, you have a negative opinion of yourself. You see yourself as undeserving. You may also believe that you're not good enough or that you don't deserve happiness and success. It's important to note that you can have high self-confidence but low self-esteem (or vice versa).

Proper Meaning and Importance of Self-Confidence

Most people think that having self-confidence is about being cocky or arrogant, but that's not always the case. Cockiness and arrogance are actually signs of low self-confidence. When you're cocky, you're trying to overcompensate for your insecurities. When you're arrogant, you're putting yourself above others to feel better about yourself. Additionally, cockiness and arrogance are usually accompanied by a fear of failure.

People who are cocky or arrogant often doubt their abilities, and they're afraid of being exposed as frauds. On the other hand, self-confidence is about having faith in your abilities. This quality is about knowing your worth and believing that you can achieve your goals. When you're self-confident, you don't compare yourself to others because you know that you're good enough just the way you are.

You're also not afraid of failure because you know you can learn from and grow from your mistakes. Lastly, self-confidence is something that you have to work on. It doesn't come naturally to everyone, and it's not a quality that you can fake. So if you want to be self-confident, put in the effort.

What Is Self-Confidence Versus Overconfidence

Distinguishing the difference between self-confidence and overconfidence is necessary. As we discussed, self-confidence is based on your abilities and merits. It means that you believe in your own abilities and have faith in your ability to achieve your goals. Overconfidence is when you overestimate your abilities and underestimate the abilities of others. This often leads to a sense of entitlement and the feeling that you don't have to work hard because you're already better than everyone else.

Overconfidence is often accompanied by arrogance, which is when you think you're better than others, and you act like it. You treat others less than you should because you know better. However, that's not what confidence is about. Even if perhaps you know you're smarter or better than someone, you still show and treat them with respect. So if you want to be self-confident, make sure that you don't fall into the trap of overconfidence.

Why Do We Need to Understand Confidence to Create a Better State of It?

If you don't understand confidence, it's hard to have self-confidence. Confidence is a quality that you build on more as you acknowledge and embrace your positive qualities. If you don't understand this, then you might struggle to develop confidence as you face adversities. Understanding confidence helps you avoid the traps of overconfidence and arrogance because you understand the proper way to embrace yourself. As mentioned earlier, overconfidence and arrogance are usually signs of low self-confidence. So if you want to be truly self-confident, make sure that you understand the proper meaning and importance of confidence.

Setting Goals and Getting Started

If you would like to be self-confident, start by setting goals. Figure out what you would like to achieve, and then plan how you're going to do it. Once you have a goal and a plan, it's time to act.

What You Need to Do

The specific goal to have in mind is: When you're working on self-improvement, it's beneficial to have specific goals in mind for yourself so that you know when it's time to cross a boundary or set a new one in your life. Furthermore, communicate this goal clearly to those around you. This will help ensure that they respect and honor the boundaries that you have set.

Make a list of goals that you want to achieve: There is no limit to what you can achieve, and setting goals is a great way to distract you from negative thoughts and motivate you to keep going. Creating goals is a great way to work on self-improvement while still keeping your boundaries in check. Perhaps you would like to try a new hobby or tackle a side hustle; setting tangible goals can help you stay on track and give you something to work towards.

Managing small portions of a big target: When it comes to setting goals, it's best to break the task into smaller and more manageable portions. This will help you feel more in control and make it easier for you to focus on the task at hand. Creating mini goals or milestones along the way as you work towards a bigger goal, may also be beneficial. This will also help you stay organized and motivated without feeling overwhelmed or discouraged. This also helps with setting boundaries because you could limit yourself to only working on the task for a certain amount of time, and that would be your boundary.

Getting Started With Creating and Developing Your Confidence Levels

As we've discussed throughout the book, our confidence levels are crucial to setting boundaries. Without confidence, we may find it difficult to set boundaries or to say "no" to people and requests. Additionally, without confidence, we may also find it difficult to pursue our goals. So, if you want to be more self-confident, it's important that you start by creating and developing your confidence levels. Below are a few tips to get you started.

Eliminating the Self-Critique

One way to develop your confidence is to eliminate negative self-criticism. Self-criticism is when we focus on our flaws and mistakes instead of our strengths and accomplishments. This can come to us as thought distortions like overgeneralization or negative self-talk, like, *I'm not good enough,* or *I can't do anything right.* If we're constantly focused on our flaws and mistakes, it's difficult to develop self-confidence because we never see ourselves in a positive light. This type of thinking can be harmful because it can prevent us from taking action and pursuing our goals.

The self-critique is the most important obstacle that you need to get rid of if you want to develop self-confidence. This type of thinking can be deeply ingrained in our minds. Additionally, like everything else in the world that follows the second law of thermodynamics, our minds have the tendency to lean towards chaos subconsciously. This makes self-criticism worse over time because, as we get older, we have more experiences to compare ourselves against.

We also have more knowledge about what other people are doing and what's possible in life. As a result, it's easy to get caught up in thinking that we're not good enough. However, it's important to start by recognizing when we're doing it. Once we're aware of when we're self-critiquing, we can then start to challenge and reframe those thoughts.

For instance, instead of thinking *I'm such a failure*, we can think, *I made a mistake, but that doesn't mean I fail at everything.* This type of thinking is called cognitive reframing. During this process, we take our negative thoughts and turn them into positive ones.

Cognitive reframing is an important tool that you can use to develop self-confidence. As we discussed in Chapter 4, overthinking can be a major problem with setting boundaries. However, cognitive reframing can teach us how to rewire our beliefs so we can focus on our positive attributes and accomplishments. Then we're prompted to take action and pursue our goals. Additionally, when we focus on our positive attributes, we're also more likely to feel good about ourselves, which can increase our motivation.

Additionally, you can try other reframing techniques, like looking at the situation from a different perspective. For example, if you're thinking *I can't do this*, try thinking, *How can I do this?* Or ask yourself, *How would [insert role model] do this?* This shift in perspective can help you see the situation in a more positive light, and it can also help you come up with creative solutions. Another reframing technique that you can use is to think about what you would say to a friend in the same situation. For example, if you're thinking *I can't do anything right*, try thinking *My friend made a mistake, but that doesn't mean they're not good at anything.* This technique can help you see the situation in a more clear light, and it can also help you be more compassionate towards yourself.

Overall, the key to eliminating self-criticism is to focus on our strengths and accomplishments instead of our flaws and mistakes. This may seem difficult at first. However, remember that we all have negative and positive qualities. Everyone makes mistakes and faces failure. The key is to learn from our mistakes and to focus on our positive attributes.

Basics of Rebuilding Self-Esteem and Self-Confidence

Rebuilding self-esteem and self-confidence can be a challenging process, as these are often areas that have been deeply impacted by past experiences. However, you can take some key steps to improve your self-esteem and confidence.

- **Believe in yourself**: Re-establishing a positive relationship with yourself is crucial to building your self-esteem. This means believing in your abilities, trusting that you have what it takes to overcome any challenges that may come your way, and accepting yourself as you are. Practicing self-compassion can also be an important part of this process, as it encourages you to be kind to yourself, rather than judging or criticizing your perceived flaws or shortcomings.

- **Set boundaries**: Another key factor in rebuilding self-confidence is learning how to set healthy and positive boundaries in all areas of your life. This may include establishing clear limits with others about what types of behaviors are acceptable for you, as well as what you will and will not tolerate. It may also be helpful to say "no" to situations that feel uncomfortable or make you feel trapped, such as in relationships with people who are emotionally abusive or manipulative.

- **Focus on the present**: Besides setting healthy boundaries, focusing on the present moment and your current experiences can improve your self-confidence. This can help you reduce negative or self-critical thoughts about the past or future. Instead, you'll be prompted to focus on what is happening in the here and now.

- **Challenge yourself**: Finally, it can also be helpful to challenge yourself and push your limits. This could involve taking on extra activities, such as learning a new skill or hobby, or engaging in more physical exercise. These types of challenges help you build resilience and practice trusting yourself in uncertain situations, which can ultimately boost your self-esteem and confidence over time.

- **Praise yourself**: An important step in rebuilding self-confidence and self-esteem is learning how to give yourself positive praise. This can involve recognizing your strengths, acknowledging your accomplishments, and celebrating the things that make you unique. One effective way to praise yourself is through regular journaling, where you reflect on your personal growth and progress over time.

- **Visualize your success and confidence**: Using visualization techniques can prompt you toward success and build confidence for the future. This involves imagining yourself as a confident, self-assured person who is proud of who you are and what you have accomplished in life. By practicing visualization regularly, you may find that it becomes more powerful and effective over time, helping you to move forward on your path to self-confidence.

Overall, whether you are looking to rebuild your self-confidence from scratch or just work on improving certain areas of it, many strategies can be helpful in this process. By believing in yourself, setting healthy boundaries, focusing on the present moment, and challenging yourself, you can begin to build a more positive relationship with yourself and foster feelings of self-confidence and self-esteem.

Creating the Wrong Image in Front of the Others

At times, people behave in a specific way just because they want to project the right image in front of others. Or, on the other hand, they may act without thinking, which may lead to unwanted perceptions from others. However, it's these qualities that prevent us from setting the proper boundaries that would prompt others to respect and perceive us in the right light.

For example, if you're constantly trying to please others by taking on more work or responsibilities than you can handle, you may set yourself up for failure. Furthermore, if your boundaries are too vague or unclear, others may feel that they don't need to adhere to them as well. This can have a negative impact on your professional reputation as well as your personal relationships.

Just Think About What You Have to Do, and Start Living That Life Inside Your Mind

When we struggle with our boundaries, it's because we're concerned about what others think or how our decisions will be received. You don't need to worry about these things as much if you stay focused on your own goals and take steps towards achieving them.

When you establish boundaries, you're fostering a prosperous life for yourself—no one else. You're living your life, so choose a life that you're happy with and that makes you feel secure. Set boundaries, create goals, and keep pushing towards success. Make sure that when you're setting boundaries for yourself, they're ones that will be beneficial for your own growth and success. Ultimately, having boundaries is important because it allows us to respect ourselves and our needs. So don't be afraid to set boundaries and stick to them—you deserve to have a life filled with peace and joy.

What Confidence Does to You

Self-confidence has several benefits. For one, it helps to increase your motivation. When you're self-confident, you're more likely to believe in your ability to achieve your goals. This belief will then motivate you to take action and to persevere even when things are tough. However, self-confidence can affect people differently. Some people have confidence in one area of their lives while lacking it in another.

To help you set goals, you need to determine how your confidence affects you and which areas you need to work on. For instance, do you need more confidence in your personal life or in your professional life? Do you need to be more confident in your relationships or in your ability to succeed in your career? Once you know the areas where you need to work, you can then set specific goals.

How Does It Matter in Your Day-To-Day Life?

We may not realize it, but our confidence levels influence our day-to-day lives. For instance, if you're not confident in your ability to do your job, you're more likely to make mistakes and underperform. On the other hand, if you're confident, you're more likely to perform well and achieve success. Additionally, confidence also affects our relationships.

If you're not confident in yourself, you're more likely to have a negative outlook on life, and you may find it difficult to trust people. The goal here is to determine how confidence levels can affect or improve your day-to-day life and to make sure that you have a healthy level of confidence. What areas in your day-to-day need improvement, and how can you cultivate those changes?

What Is the Fine Line Between Confidence and Self-Confidence?

There is a fine line between confidence and self-confidence. Confidence is when you believe in your ability to do something. Self-confidence is when you believe in your ability to do something and also have the motivation to take action. For example, with confidence, you may believe that you can do your job, but you're not motivated to take action. With self-confidence, you not only believe that you can successfully complete your job, but you're also motivated to take action, like applying for a promotion or asking for a raise.

Mistakes to Avoid

We're humans, and occasionally we make mistakes. Listed below are a few common mistakes to avoid that can affect your self-esteem.

Modern Social Media and Internet Might Be Deceiving You Totally

In the modern world, social media and the internet are powerful tools. It can spread positivity, but also deceive people. People use it as a platform for comparison and oversharing information that causes distress for others. This type of "influencing" does not promote healthy boundaries or lifestyles; instead, it creates an environment where people feel the need to be perfect.

Additionally, the social media settings and layout are specifically designed to keep people engaged, promoting the unrealistic idea that life should be perfect and everyone should strive for perfection. This is not the case, and it's important to remember that real-life boundaries are set by you, not by what someone else tells you or expects of you. Having boundaries is about respecting yourself, and that doesn't mean that you should be limited to what society expects of you. Set boundaries for yourself and make sure that they are beneficial for your own growth and success.

Avoid the "Social Media Influencers"

Falling into the social media trap of comparing yourself with those who appear to be living a life of perfection can be too easy. However, not everything you see is reality, and it's detrimental to your own boundaries if you compare your life with someone else's. This can lead you down a path of frustration and low self-esteem, which is not a healthy space to be in. So instead of comparing yourself, focus on your own goals and achievements; this will help you find the motivation and encouragement you need to keep setting healthy boundaries for yourself.

Don't Believe Everything That You Read on the Internet

Be aware of the information that you're reading, especially when it comes to the internet. Many articles and websites offer advice, but many are not reliable or applicable in every situation. Take what you read with a grain of salt, and instead focus on your own needs and feelings.

Avoid Pushing Yourself More Than What You Can Take

Do not push yourself beyond what you can handle. Raising your goals or taking on new challenges is a great way to improve your skills. However, taking on too much can lead to more stress and harm than good. Setting boundaries that are too strict, or setting goals that are too high, will only lead to frustration. Concentrate on goals that are realistic.

When you push yourself too hard, it can lead to burnout, and you won't be able to make progress or achieve your goals. This can lead to a vicious cycle of feeling overwhelmed and underachieving, so focus on setting boundaries and goals that are achievable. This will help you stay motivated and reach success in a healthier way.

What Is Your True Potential?

Your true potential is what you're capable of if you reach it. This means becoming the best version of yourself that you can be in all areas of your life. To reach your full potential, you need to focus on personal growth. You develop your potential as you continuously work on becoming a better version of yourself. This quality is about expanding your knowledge, learning new skills, and improving your mind, body, and soul.

So, how do you become the best version of yourself?

The answer is simple: By taking action.

You need to take steps every day to improve yourself. This might mean reading self-help books, working out, meditating, or practicing mindfulness. It's up to you to decide what you need to do to grow. But the most important thing is to take action and not just sit around and wait for things to happen.

Remember, you have the power to change your life. You have the power to reach your full potential. All it takes is some effort and determination.

The Destructive Emotional Baggage

We all have emotional baggage from our past. This might include things like trauma, pain, hurt, or anger. This emotional baggage can hold us back and prevent us from reaching our full potential.

To get rid of this emotional baggage, we need to first notice it. Once we're aware of it, we can start working on letting it go. Emotional baggage can come to us in many forms. It might be something that we're holding on to from our past, or it might be something that's happening in our present.

To let go of emotional baggage, we need to work on forgiving ourselves and others. Forgiveness is an important step in healing old wounds. Letting go of the need for revenge is also critical. This doesn't mean that we forget what happened to us. It means that we choose to move on and not let the past define our present or future. This means accepting that you've made mistakes and that you're not perfect. Forgiveness is about giving yourself grace and understanding.

We can also work on changing our beliefs about ourselves. If we have negative beliefs about ourselves, they'll hold us back from reaching our full potential. So, it's important to identify these negative beliefs and work on changing them.

Lastly, we need to practice self-love. This means accepting ourselves, flaws and all. We practice being kind and compassionate to ourselves. We provide ourselves with the same love and understanding that we would give to others.

Accepting ourselves is an important step in reaching our full potential. When we love and accept ourselves, we open up the possibility of becoming the best version of ourselves. You can practice acceptance by meditating, practicing mindfulness, or journaling.

Releasing the Need for Perfection

A large barrier that stops us from reaching our full potential is the need for perfection. We live in a world that's obsessed with perfection. We're constantly bombarded with images of perfect bodies, perfect lives, and perfect homes. This can make us feel like we're not good enough. It can make us feel like we need to be perfect to be happy and successful.

The need for perfection is a destructive force. This quality holds us back and prevents us from reaching our full potential. When we're focused on being perfect, we're not focused on becoming the best version of ourselves. We're not focused on growth or improvement. Instead, we're focused on staying the same. Being a perfectionist is not always easy to overcome, but by improving your self-esteem and setting healthy boundaries with yourself, you can start to let go of the need for perfection.

Three Steps to Take Right Now to Reach Your Full Potential

If you're ready to start working on reaching your full potential, here are three steps you can take right now:

1. **Set some goals.**

Think about what you want to achieve. What do you want to accomplish in the next year? The next five years? Write down your goals and make a plan for how you're going to achieve them.

2. **Work on your mindset.**

Your mindset plays a big role in determining whether or not you reach your full potential. If you have a growth mindset, you believe that you can improve and grow. Mistakes are part of the journey. You're not afraid to take risks. You're open to learning new things.

3. **Take action.**

No matter how big or small your goals are, taking action is the only way to achieve them. So, start taking steps today to reach your full potential. Read books, listen to podcasts, take courses, and do whatever else you need to do to grow and improve. Remember, progress is never linear. There will be ups and downs. But as long as you keep taking action, you will eventually reach your goals.

Getting Cured of the Desire of People Pleasing

We live in a world where we're constantly bombarded with messages telling us we need to be a certain way to be accepted. We're told that we need to look a certain way, act a certain way, and think a certain way. It can make us feel like we need to change ourselves to be accepted.

To overcome people pleasing, you can

- set boundaries with yourself and others.
- work on your self-esteem.
- practice accepting yourself.
- reframe the thoughts that cause you to please others
- release the need for perfectionism.

Be Open to Making and Learning From Mistakes

Making mistakes is a natural part of life. It's how we learn and grow. But many of us are afraid to make mistakes because we're afraid of being judged or rejected. We're afraid of looking foolish. We're afraid of failing.

Be open to making and learning from mistakes. Being imperfect is something you need to be okay with. You need to be okay with looking foolish. You need to be okay with failing. Remember, progress is never linear. There will be ups and downs. The downs can be powerful and hurtful, but they can also be the catalyst for growth—the secret behind this is our mindset, as we discussed earlier in the chapter.

Be open to making and learning from mistakes. Embrace your imperfections. Be okay with looking foolish. Be okay with failing, and most importantly, be comfortable taking action.

Eliminate Any Existing Phobia or Doubt

One of the best things we can do to reach our full potential is to eliminate any existing doubts or fears. We all have doubts and fears. But when they're holding us back from taking action, they need to go.

To overcome your doubts and fears, you can:

- Get clear on what you want: When your mind is filled with doubts and fears, it's hard to see what you really want. So, take some time to get clear on your goals. What do you want to achieve? Why do you want to achieve it?

- Identify your doubts and fears: Once you know what you want, determine your doubts and fears. What's holding you back?

- Challenge your doubts and fears: After you've identified your doubts and fears, it's time to challenge them. Are they true? Do they make sense?

- Take action despite your doubts and fears: The only way to overcome your doubts and fears is to take action despite them. It won't be easy. But it's the only way to achieve your goals.

Keep Moving Forward

No matter where you are in life, keep moving forward. Don't let your past define you. Don't let your mistakes hold you back. And don't let your doubts and fears control you. If you allow these negative qualities to control you, you won't be able to create the life that you want and deserve. Setting boundaries is an important part of making sure you stay on track. Boundaries help protect you from people and situations that can derail your progress. They give you a sense of control over your environment, helping to reduce stress and free up your mental energy for more meaningful and productive tasks.

By cultivating a sense of boundaries in your life, you'll find that you're better able to keep moving forward, no matter what life throws at you. Creating boundaries is not always easy—it takes practice to recognize where your limits are and understand how those limits should be respected. But if you invest the time and energy to develop healthy boundaries, you'll find that it's worthwhile.

With boundaries in place, you can move forward with confidence and security, knowing that your limits are being honored and respected by others. Setting boundaries will help you live a peaceful life—one where you can focus on the important things and live in harmony. You have the power to create the life you want.

Chapter 10:

Developing a Growth Mindset

Now that we understand how vital our mindset is to developing healthy boundaries, let's examine what the right mindset looks like.

Learn to Think How You Want to Be, Not How You Are

Take a moment to consider the current thoughts you carry around with you every day. What kinds of things do you tell yourself? Are your thoughts positive or negative? Do they inspire you to take action, or do they hold you back?

Your current mindset is likely the result of years of conditioning from your family, friends, society, and even the media. And while some of these outside influences may have been helpful, others may have led you astray.

Our thoughts and actions are closely linked. In many cases, it's solely your thought process that's holding you back from taking the actions you need to in order to achieve your goals. As the saying goes, "If you think you can, or you think you can't, you're right."

So, if you want to change your actions, you need to start by changing your thoughts.

Developing the Best Mindset Is Actually Depending Only on Your Willpower

Your thoughts are solely under your control. No one can make you think a certain way against your will. Therefore, if you want to develop the right mindset, it's entirely up to you.

Of course, this isn't always easy. Our thoughts are often influenced by our emotions, which can be hard to control. However, with practice, it is possible to develop a more positive outlook on life, even in the face of adversity.

Fixed Versus Growth Mindset

One of the most important things to understand about mindset is the difference between a fixed mindset and a growth mindset.

People with a fixed mindset believe that their abilities and talents are static. They think they are either born with certain gifts or they're not, and there's nothing they can do to change it. This often leads them to give up easily because they feel like they can't improve.

On the other hand, people with a growth mindset believe that their abilities can be developed over time. They are always looking for ways to learn and grow, and they see mistakes as learning opportunities rather than failures. This allows them to approach life with a more positive attitude and to persevere even when things are tough.

Which Mindset Do You Have?

Think about how you currently approach your goals and challenges. Do you believe you can improve with time and effort, or do you think that your current abilities are set in stone? If it's the latter, then it's time to start thinking differently.

Some helpful tips for developing the right mindset include:

- Be mindful of your thoughts. Pay attention to the thoughts you're having on a daily basis. Are they mostly negative or positive? If you think negative thoughts more often than you'd like, try to reframe them in a more positive light.

- Challenge your negative thoughts. When you catch yourself thinking something negative, take a moment to question it. Is there any evidence to support this thought? Is it really true? Or is it just a harmful belief that you've been carrying around for years?

- Surround yourself with positive people. The people you spend time with can have a big impact on your thoughts and emotions. If you're surrounded by negativity, it will be hard to maintain a positive outlook. Try to spend time with people who make you feel good and who support your goals.

- Be patient with yourself. Change doesn't happen overnight. It takes time and effort to develop a better mindset. Be patient with yourself and don't expect perfection. Every step in the right direction is a success.

Developing the right mindset is essential for achieving any goal, big or small. By taking the time to change your thoughts, you can change your life. It all starts with a single thought. So, why not make it a positive one?

How to Create a Proper Sense of What You Want to Be and Get Into the Right Mindset

Creating a sense of what you want to be is the first step in getting into the right mindset. This can be done by setting goals and visualizing what you want to achieve. Visualization techniques, like visualization boards and mental rehearsal, can be helpful in this process. Once you have a clear sense of what you want to achieve, you can then develop a plan to get there.

This may involve studying, networking, or taking classes. However, no one achieves their goals overnight. It takes time, effort, and perseverance. Additionally, keep your expectations realistic. This means that you shouldn't set unrealistic timelines or expect no setbacks. Setbacks are a normal part of the process, and they can actually help you learn and grow.

Developing a positive mindset is also crucial. This means focusing on the things that you can control and believing in yourself. When you have a positive mindset, you're more likely to take action and achieve your goals.

In conclusion, self-confidence is an important part of achieving success. However, it's something that we have to work on developing.

The Mindset of Practicality

A practical mindset is essential for achieving success. This means focusing on the parts of life that you can control and taking action. For example, if you're working on a project with a team at work, you can't control what everyone else does, but you can control your own work. Similarly, if you're trying to lose weight, you can't control how fast your body loses weight or even where you lose weight, but you can control what you eat and how much you exercise.

When you have a practical mindset, you focus on the things that you can control and take action. This means that you don't waste time worrying about things that you can't control. Instead, you focus on the things that you can do to achieve your goals. Additionally, a practical mindset also means having realistic expectations.

How to Prime Your Mindset for Incredible Success

Success starts with your mindset. If you want to be successful, you need to think like one. That means having faith in your abilities, setting goals, and taking action. It also means surrounding yourself with positive people and staying away from negative influences.

Unlocking the Natural Success Mindset

Unlocking your potential and mindset begins with understanding your success triggers. These are the things that motivate you and help you stay focused on your goals. When you know what your success triggers are, you can use them to prime your mindset for success.

Some common success triggers include:

- **A sense of purpose**: When you have a clear sense of why you're doing something, it's much easier to stay motivated.

- **A growth mindset**: People with a growth mindset believe that they can improve with effort. This type of thinking is linked to greater success in life.

- **Positive reinforcement**: When you get positive feedback from others, it reinforces your beliefs about yourself and your abilities.

- **A sense of control**: When you feel like you're in control of your life, you're more likely to be successful.

- **A support network**: Having a supportive network of friends and family can help you reach your goals.

To unlock these triggers in your own life, start by taking some time to reflect on what has helped you succeed in the past. Once you know what your success triggers are, make a conscious effort to incorporate them into your life.

Winning the Battle for Control Inside Your Mind

An important aspect of success is feeling like you're in control of your life. When you feel like you're in control, you're more likely to take risks and go after your goals.

There are two main types of control: External and internal. External control is when you feel like you have to take action in order to achieve a certain outcome. This type of control often leads to anxiety and stress. Internal control is when you feel like you're in control of your own life and destiny. This type of control is linked to greater happiness and success.

To increase your sense of internal control, start by taking some time to reflect on the areas of your life that are most important to you. Then, attempt to focus on what's within your control. Let go of any need to control every aspect of your life. Accepting that some things are out of your control can help you relax and enjoy life more.

To create an external sense of control, you can start by making a list of goals or situations that are valuable to you. Then, make a plan for how you're going to achieve them. For example, if you want to get a promotion, make a plan to network with people in your field and to brush up on your skills. Or, if you want to lose weight, make a plan to eat healthy and exercise regularly.

However, this battle that takes place inside your mind can only be one if you let it be. If you instead focus on the things that are in your control and work on building a growth mindset, success will come much easier.

Getting Rid of Bad Programming Inside Your Brain and Negative Emotions

Bad programming inside your brain causes poor decisions. This includes negative thinking, self-doubt, and negative emotions.

These negative qualities can hold you back and prevent you from reaching your potential. To get rid of them, you need to notice when they're happening. Once you're aware of them, you can work on changing your thinking.

One way to change your thinking is to focus on the positive. This means looking for the good in every situation and choosing to see the glass as half full. When you focus on the positive, you'll notice that your thinking changes.

Another way to change your thinking is to challenge your negative thoughts. When you have a negative thought, ask yourself if it's really true. If it's not, let it go. If it is true, ask yourself what you can do to change the situation.

You can also work on changing your emotions by practicing gratitude. When you're feeling down, take a moment to think about things that you're thankful for. This will help shift your focus and improve your mood.

Finally, it's important to practice self-compassion. This means being kind to yourself when you make mistakes. It's normal to make mistakes—we all do it. What's important is how you handle it. If you're hard on yourself, you'll only make things worse. But if you're gentle and understanding with yourself, you'll be able to move on and learn from your mistakes.

Developing Your Natural Success Mindset

Success is a mindset. Success is a way of thinking and approaching life that allows you to tap into your full potential. To be triumphant, you need to develop a success mindset. But what exactly is a success mindset?

A success mindset is the belief that you can achieve anything you set your mind to. You have faith in yourself and your abilities. You know and understand that you can reach your goals, no matter how difficult they may seem. The good news is, success is a choice. Anyone can develop a success mindset if they're willing to put in the effort.

Here are some tips for developing a success mindset:

- **Accept that intelligence can be developed**. Just because you're not a genius doesn't mean you can't become one. With enough effort, anyone can increase their intelligence and abilities.

- **Believe in yourself**. The first step to having a success mindset is believing that you can achieve success. You need to have faith in yourself and your abilities. When you believe in yourself, anything becomes possible.

- **Set your sights high**. Don't be afraid to set your sights high and reach for the stars. When you aim for big goals, you'll be surprised at what you can achieve.

- **Be persistent**. Never give up on your dreams. No matter how many times you fail, get back up and try again. Only through persistence will you achieve success.

- **Stay positive**. When things get tough, it's important to stay positive. Believe in yourself and remember why you're doing what you're doing. A positive attitude is essential for keeping your motivation high.

- **Learn from your mistakes**. Everyone makes mistakes, but it's important to learn from them. When you make a mistake, take the time to figure out what went wrong and how you can avoid making the same mistake in the future.

- **Be resilient**. Resilience is key to success. No matter how many setbacks you face, don't give up. Keep moving forward and never give up on your dreams.

The Power of Authenticity

People often ask me how I've been able to achieve the level of success that I have. And while many factors have contributed to my success, one of the most important is authenticity.

Being authentic means being true to yourself. It means living your life in a way that's authentic to you. It means being honest about your thoughts, feelings, and experiences.

When you're authentic, you're not pretending to be someone you're not. You're not trying to impress others or live up to their expectations. You're simply being yourself. The benefits of authenticity are many. When you're authentic, you have a deep sense of self-awareness. You know who you are, what you stand for, and what you want out of life.

Being authentic also allows you to build deeper, more meaningful relationships. When you're genuine with others, they're more likely to be genuine with you, and when people know they can trust you, they're more likely to confide in you.

To be successful in life, it's essential that you be authentic. People can see through phoniness and insincerity. So if you want to build trust and create meaningful connections, you need to be real.

The Carefree Operating System Inside Your Brain

The operating system inside your brain is designed for success. This structure is called the reticular activating system, and its job is to help you achieve your goals.

The reticular activating system filters information and focuses your attention on what's most important. When you're trying to develop a mindset, it's important to program your reticular activating system appropriately.

Here's how you can do it:

- **Define your goals**. The first step is to clearly define your goals. What do you want to achieve? What are your long-term and short-term goals? When you have a clear vision of what you want, you can start to program your reticular activating system to help you achieve it.

- **Visualize your goals**. Once you've defined your goals, it's important to visualize them. See yourself achieving your goals in your mind's eye. The more vividly you visualize your success, the more likely you are to achieve it.

- **Take action steps**. Identify the steps you need to take to achieve your goals, and then take them. The more action you take, the more likely you are to achieve your goals.

- **Be patient**. It takes time to program your reticular activating system for success. Be patient and don't get discouraged if you don't see results immediately. Keep taking action, and eventually, you'll achieve the success you desire.

- **Believe in yourself**. The ultimate step is to believe in yourself. You need to believe that you can achieve your goals. When you have faith in yourself, anything is possible.

Additional tips include:

- **Embrace challenges**: When you face a challenge, it activates your reticular activating system and programs it for success. When you're presented with a challenge, your brain searches for solutions. It looks for resources and information that can help you overcome the challenge. Searching and learning help you grow and develop new skills.

- **Take risks**: When you're willing to take risks, it shows your brain that you're committed to achieving your goals. Taking risks also allows you to learn and grow. When you try new things, you expand your horizons and open yourself up to new possibilities.

- **Be persistent**: When you're working towards your goals, there will be setbacks and obstacles. Prompt yourself to persevere through these tough times. When you're persistent, it shows your brain that you're committed, which programs your reticular activating system for success.

- **Determine your strengths or weaknesses**: Knowing your strengths and weaknesses can help you program your reticular activating system. When you're aware of your strengths, you can use them to your advantage. And when you're aware of your weaknesses, you can work on improving them. This self-awareness allows you to focus on what's most important and achieve success.

- **Review the success of others**: To program this system, you can also learn from the success of others. When you see someone else achieve success, it activates your reticular activating system and programs it for success. When you see someone else achieve their goals, it shows you that it's possible. It gives you proof that your goals are attainable.

- **Seek feedback**: When you get feedback, it helps you understand what's working and what's not. This feedback allows you to adjust your actions and improve your chances of success.

By taking action and believing in yourself, you can achieve any goal you desire.

How to Get What You Really Want

Communicating effectively is crucial for success. When you can express yourself clearly and confidently, you're more likely to get what you want.

Here are some tips for communicating effectively:

- **Be clear about what you want**. The first step is to be clear about what you want. What is your goal? What do you want to achieve? When you're clear about your goals, you can communicate them more effectively.

- **Be confident**. Confidence is important when communicating with others. If you're not sure of yourself, it will be difficult to get what you want. Believe in yourself and your ability to communicate effectively.

- **Be assertive**. Do not be aggressive—be assertive. You need to stand up for yourself and be firm in your convictions. However, at the same time, you don't want to come across as pushy or demanding. Tips on how to be assertive:

- **Listen more than you talk**. When you're engaged in a conversation, listen more than you talk. When you're trying to communicate with someone, you need to hear what they're saying. Only then can you respond effectively.

- **Use "I" statements**. When you're communicating, use "I" statements. For example, say "I want" or "I need." This will help the other person understand your perspective.

- **Be respectful**. Show others respect when you're communicating with someone else. Even if you don't agree with them, you should still treat them with respect.

- **Keep it simple**. When you're communicating, try to keep your message simple. Don't use big words or technical jargon. The simpler you can make it, the better.

- **Be patient**. Don't rush someone or try to force them to understand your point of view. Be patient. If you're patient, they'll be more likely to listen to you.

- **Be positive**. When you're positive, it's easier for others to understand and accept what you're saying. You can come across as reasonable and many people will work with you. If you come across demanding, then they might think you're mean and avoid you.

- **Practice**. The best way to become a better communicator is to practice. Talk to friends, family, and strangers.

Living Life on Your Purpose (That Actually Matters)

If you want to live a life that actually matters, you need to find your purpose. What is your calling? What are you meant to do with your life?

Your purpose is the reason you're here. It's what you're supposed to do with your life.

There are many ways to find your purpose. Below are a few.

Follow your passion: One way to find your purpose is to follow your passion. What are you passionate about? What makes you feel alive? When you're doing what you love, it's easy to stay motivated and focused.

Help others: Lending a helping hand can help you figure out what your core values are. What can you do to make a difference in the world? When you're helping others, you're fulfilling your purpose.

Do what you're good at: Soul-searching and determining what you're good at can be another way to find purpose in life. What are your strengths and talents? When you use your strengths and talents to help others, you're fulfilling your purpose.

Be yourself: Be true to who you are. When you're being yourself, you're living on purpose.

Live in the present moment: When you're living in the present moment, you're not worrying about the past or the future. You're living in the now.

Create a personal vision statement: A vision statement can help you determine your purpose. This statement includes what you want to achieve in your life and your values. Your vision statement should be specific, positive, and realistic. For example, your vision statement could be:

- "I want to make a difference in the world by helping others."
- "I want to be a successful writer and inspire others with my words."
- "I want to be a teacher and help others learn and grow."

Whatever your vision is, make sure it's something you're passionate about. Something that will make you want to get out of bed every day and live your life to the fullest.

Practice gratitude: When you feel negative thoughts creeping in, try to counter them with thoughts of gratitude. What are some things in your life that you're thankful for? Focusing on the positive can help offset the negative. When you're grateful for what you have, you're more likely to find your purpose. Gratitude can help you see the good in your life and appreciate what you have. It can also help you let go of negativity and focus on what's important.

Join a community: When you join a community, you're surrounded by people with similar interests and goals. This can help you find your purpose. When you're around others who are living their purpose, it's easier to see what's possible for your own life. You can also learn from their example and get support and encouragement from them.

Read often: Reading can help you find your purpose. When you read, you're exposed to new ideas and ways of thinking. This can help you see things in a different light and find your own path in life.

Find a role model or inspiration: When you're trying to find your purpose, it's helpful to find someone to look up to. Someone who's already living their purpose. Someone who can inspire you and show you what's possible. When you find someone to look up to, pay attention to how they live their life. What do they do on a daily basis? What are their values and priorities? How do they treat others?

Practice self-acceptance: When you accept yourself, you're more likely to find your purpose. Self-acceptance means accepting yourself for who you are. It means valuing and respecting yourself. It means being kind and compassionate to yourself. You will be more likely to be authentic and true to yourself. You're also more likely to find your purpose.

No matter what your purpose is, it's important to live life on purpose. When you're living on purpose, you're fulfilled and happy.

The Natural Abundance

When we think of abundance, we often think of money, possessions, or success. But abundance is so much more than that. Abundance is a state of mind. It's a way of living.

Abundance is about having a plethora of love, joy, and happiness in your life. It's about having an abundance of good health, good relationships, and fulfilling work. Abundance is about living life to the fullest. It's about being present and grateful for what you have. It's about having faith that there's more than enough for everyone.

When you live in abundance, you open yourself up to limitless possibilities. You see that there's more than enough for you and everyone else. You trust that the universe is abundant and supports you. Abundance is not a competition. There's enough for everyone. So, there's no need to compete or compare yourself to others.

The Power of Shifting Perspective

When it comes to abundance, perspective is everything. The way you see the world dictates how you live your life.

If you have a scarcity mindset, you believe that there's not enough for everyone. You think that there's only so much to go around, and so you compete with others for what's available. If you have an abundance mindset, you believe that there's more than enough for everyone. You know that there's an unlimited supply of resources and opportunities. And so, you share what you have with others.

The key to living an abundant life is to shift your perspective from one of scarcity to one of abundance. When you do, your whole life will change.

Here are some ways to shift your perspective:

- **Start each day by listing five things you're grateful for**: You can be grateful for your health, your family, your friends, your work, or anything else that brings you joy. Gratitude attracts more of what you're grateful for into your life.

- **Visualize abundance**: Another way to shift your perspective is to visualize abundance. When you visualize abundance, you see that there's more than enough for everyone.

    - To do this, close your eyes and imagine a world where there's plenty of everything for everyone. See yourself living in abundance. Feel the joy and happiness that comes with it.

    - Then, open your eyes and take a few deep breaths. Let the feeling of abundance wash over you.

- **Change your language**: The way you speak reflects your mindset. So if you want to change your mindset, change your language.

- Instead of saying, “I can't afford it,” say, “How can I afford it?” Instead of saying, “I don't have enough time,” say, “How can I make time for it?” When you change your language, you change your mindset. And when you change your mindset, you change your life.

Final Thoughts

And that's it! You've finished the last chapter in *Setting Healthy Boundaries*. Remember that setting boundaries is all about respecting yourself and taking ownership of your own life. Set goals, break them down into smaller portions to feel more in control, and ultimately keep pushing towards success and a life that is filled with peace and joy.

Stand tall and say no if you have to, and remember that having boundaries is an integral part of self-care. Believe in yourself and trust your intuition—you know what's best for you. Setting boundaries is a process that takes time and effort, but it will be worth it in the end. Boundaries can be intimidating, but once you set them, there's nothing stopping you from achieving greatness! So take care of yourself and make sure to set those healthy boundaries!

Conclusion

Congratulations! You have completed *Setting Healthy Boundaries*. Were you able to pinpoint which boundaries you were lacking? Have you determined which boundaries you want to implement in order to create healthier relationships? Are you ready to work on setting some new boundaries in your life?

When I first realized which boundaries I needed, I remember feeling an enormous wave of relief. I felt more assured. But then a moment of panic set in as I realized I had to actually start setting boundaries. That would also mean people in my life wouldn't be too thrilled with me at first. I was afraid of being rejected and alone.

The key is to remember that your boundaries are for you. They are not to control or manipulate others, but rather to protect yourself and give yourself a sense of peace. Some people may push back at first. But that's okay! You have a right to protect yourself, and if someone can't respect your boundaries, then they are not worth your time and energy.

When you have boundaries, you are in control of your life. You get to decide what is and isn't acceptable to you. You get to choose how you want to be treated. Other people won't be able to take advantage of you or control you. You'll be able to create healthy and fulfilling relationships.

Here is a brief reminder of the tools you learned in the book:

- Your boundaries should come from a place of self-respect and not to control or manipulate others

- To set a boundary, you need to be clear about what your needs are and be confident in saying no

- You can set boundaries by saying no, walking away, or using body language

- To set and maintain boundaries, you need self-confidence and self-esteem. You can develop these qualities by identifying your strengths, practicing self-compassion, and speaking kindly to yourself.

- Your triggers play a crucial role in setting boundaries. By understanding your triggers, you can avoid getting overwhelmed and maintain control in difficult situations.

- You can pinpoint your triggers by keeping a journal, practicing self-awareness, and being mindful of your thoughts and emotions.

- Communicate your boundaries to others in a clear and concise way. You can do this by using "I" statements, speaking calmly, and avoiding blame.

These tools will help you set boundaries in all areas of your life—with friends, family, co-workers, and even strangers. Remember to take small, baby steps at first. Over time, setting boundaries will become easier and more second nature to you as you gain more confidence in yourself.

Most importantly, give yourself grace during this process. This is unfamiliar territory for you, and it takes time to make lasting changes. Be patient with yourself and others, and soon you'll be living a life with healthy boundaries!

Remember, you deserve to be respected, and you have a right to set boundaries. So go out there and start creating healthy relationships! If you found this book helpful, please share it with a friend or family member who may benefit from reading it. Thank you for reading! Wishing you all the best in your journey of setting healthy boundaries. Also, please leave a review on Amazon.com (use link or QRcode):

https://www.amazon.com/review/create-review?&asin=8797430609

References

Better Health Channel. (2012). *Self esteem.* Vic.gov.au. https://www.betterhealth.vic.gov.au/health/healthyliving/self-esteem

Boundaries: What are they and how to create them | Wellness Center | University of Illinois Chicago. (2022, February 25). Wellnesscenter.uic.edu. https://wellnesscenter.uic.edu/news-stories/boundaries-what-are-they-and-how-to-create-them/

Casabianca, S. (2021, May 6). *15 Cognitive Distortions to Blame for Your Negative Thinking.* Psych Central. https://psychcentral.com/lib/cognitive-distortions-negative-thinking

Cherry, K. (2021, July 20). *What Exactly Is Self-Esteem?* Verywell Mind. https://www.verywellmind.com/what-is-self-esteem-2795868

Chua, C. (2010, April 2). *42 Practical Ways To Improve Yourself.* Lifehack. https://www.lifehack.org/articles/lifestyle/42-practical-ways-to-improve-yourself.html

Cook, A. (2018, October 11). *4 ways to shift from overthinking to courageous risk-taking.* Dr. Alison Cook. https://www.dralisoncook.com/how-to-move-from-overthinking-to-courageous-risk-taking/

Davis, T. (2019, April 11). *15 Ways to Build a Growth Mindset.* Psychology Today. https://www.psychologytoday.com/us/blog/click-here-happiness/201904/15-ways-build-growth-mindset

Five steps to help build and strengthen your confidence. (2010, August 5). Tanveer Naseer. https://tanveernaseer.com/5-steps-to-help-build-and-strengthen-your-confidence/

Garden Gate Staff. (2019, March 12). *Meet 12 of the Best Container Plants.* Garden Gate. https://www.gardengatemagazine.com/articles/containers/all/meet-8-of-the-best-container-plants/

Lolly Daskal. (2017, January 9). *19 Simple Ways to Boost Your Self-Esteem Quickly.* Inc. https://www.inc.com/lolly-daskal/19-simple-ways-to-boost-your-self-esteem-quickly.html

Raising low self-esteem. (2021, February 1). Nhs.uk. https://www.nhs.uk/mental-health/self-help/tips-and-support/raise-low-self-esteem/

Noyes, A. (2020, September 28). *Potted Shade Flowers: 20 Great Shade-Loving Plants For Containers.* Gardening Chores. https://www.gardeningchores.com/container-plants-for-shade/

Palmer, H. (2021, November 1). *8 self-improvement tips to get your life back on track.* Family Builders. https://familybuildersok.org/2021/11/eight-self-improvement-tips-to-get-your-life-back-on-track/

Pattemore, C. (2021, June 3). *10 Ways to Build and Preserve Better Boundaries.* Psych Central. https://psychcentral.com/lib/10-way-to-build-and-preserve-better-boundaries

Salleh, M. R. (2008). Life event, stress and illness. *The Malaysian Journal of Medical Sciences, 15*(4), 9–18. https://www.ncbi.nlm.nih.gov/pmc/articles/PMC3341916/

Shrikant, A. (2022, August 19). *Setting healthy boundaries with your partner will only make your relationship stronger, says therapist—here's how to get started.* CNBC. https://www.cnbc.com/2022/08/18/how-to-set-healthy-boundaries-in-your-relationship.html

Weir, K. (2020, April 1). Nurtured by nature. *American Psychological Association.* https://www.apa.org/monitor/2020/04/nurtured-nature

Wooll, M. (2021, October 19). *Start finding your purpose and unlock your best life.* Betterup. https://www.betterup.com/blog/finding-purpose

What is a growth mindset and how can you develop one? (2022, April 25). FutureLearn. https://www.futurelearn.com/info/blog/general/develop-growth-mindset

Printed in Great Britain
by Amazon

59671800R00076